HOW PEOPLE CHANGE

The essay "How People Change" first appeared in *Commentary*. In a different form it is included in this work, which bears its name.

Portions appeared in *The Desert* by Allen Wheelis. Reprinted by permission of Basic Books, Inc. Copyright © 1969, 1970 by Allen Wheelis.

"Grass" is reprinted from *The Quest for Identity* by Allen Wheelis, by permission of W. W. Norton & Company, Inc. Copyright © 1958 by W. W. Norton & Company, Inc.

A hardcover edition of this book is published by Harper & Row, Publishers, Inc.

First HARPER COLOPHON edition published 1975

ISBN: 0-06-090447-X

Designed by Sidney Feinberg

05   RRD-H 40 39 38 37 36

HOW
PEOPLE
CHANGE

Allen Wheelis

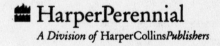
HarperPerennial
A Division of HarperCollinsPublishers

Contents

I

SUFFERING

WE have not far to look for suffering. It's in the streets, fills the air, lies upon our friends. Faces of pain look at us from newspaper, from TV screen. We know them: black man swinging in the warm wind, sealed cattle cars rumbling through the bitter cold, the glare of Auschwitz at midnight, the sweet smell.

And then there's always the suffering inside. But that's different. It may be very bad, this private misery, but different.

For many people pain is imposed, there's no escape. It may be impersonal, unavoidable, as by fire, flood, cancer; or man-made, as in wars, sack of cities, rape of girls. Victims still have choice; there's always a little corner of freedom. They may throw spears at the bombers or bow in prayer, may curse or plead; but they may not choose to suffer or not suffer. That choice has been foreclosed. Starving blacks of Biafra scrounge for roots, fight each other for rats; Vietnamese children with melted flesh wander homeless, orphaned, across a lunar desert.

Many of us have never known this kind of misery, have never felt a lash or club, never been shot at, persecuted,

3

bombed, starved—yet we suffer too. Wealth and intelligence and good fortune are no protection. Having had good parents helps but guarantees nothing; misery comes equally to high born and low, comes with the gold spoon, to prince and princess and ladies-in-waiting, to groom and gamekeeper, to the mighty and the humble. We feel our suffering as alien, desperately unwanted, yet nothing imposes it. We eat, often exceedingly well; the roof over our head is timber and tile; we know deep carpets, thin china, great music, rare wine; someone looks at us with love; we have friends, families; our needs are met. In some way, unnoticed, unknown, we must elect our suffering, create it. It may be quite intense.

Some of it is public knowledge—madness, suicide, running amuck. Some of it is visible only to a few, to family and friends who see the withdrawal, depression, the sense of rejection, the clawing competitiveness, the bitter frustration, bafflement and anger, year after year after year. At the concert or opera, walking about in the lobby, we bow, we smile, we glitter—show nothing of the misery inside. And some of our suffering is altogether private, known to no one but he who suffers, not even the one asleep beside him, is borne with shame as some indescribable awkwardness in living, a kind of disloyalty to life to be in despair in the midst of plenty.

Imposed suffering takes priority over elected suffering, as material needs take precedence over spiritual. "First feed the belly, then talk right and wrong," says Mac the Knife. Or Sartre: ". . . the exploitation of men by other men, undernourishment—these make metaphysical unhappiness a luxury and relegate it to second place. Hunger—now that *is* an evil." Imposed suffering, therefore, protects from the elected kind, crowds it out. We simply cannot create despair from subjective roots if we are forced into despair by persecution. In the concentration camp, states of created despair are remembered vaguely as if from a different life, discontinuous with the present one in which despair issues from S.S. truncheons.

To those whose suffering is imposed, elected suffering seems unreal. Lacking in measurable circumstance, in objective explanation, it seems illusory, made up, "in the head." Victims of the whip feel envy of those so sheltered from pain as to be able to dream up states of misery; contempt when such fortunate ones have the arrogance to elegize their torment; a hateful mirth at existential despair hatching in a nest of IBM stock certificates.

We who compose our own misery are ambivalent toward victims of imposed suffering. We feel a subtle pride— secret, never expressed, unknown often even to ourselves —that our misery is more complicated, spiritual; as if we whispered, "The pain of being hungry, of being beaten, is very bad, we sympathize, will make a contribution to CARE; but it is, after all, a primitive suffering; anyone can feel it; just leave them alone, give them enough to eat, and they'd be happy—whereas only a poet could feel what I feel." At the same time, more openly felt, more easily expressed, we feel shame, judge our created misery to be petty in comparison.

In fact they are equally bad: depression or starvation is a hard choice; the terror of the ledge ten floors up matches the terror of the firing squad. In felt experience, that is: in worthiness we cannot call them equal. We who compose our own misery are ashamed at Babi Yar, at Nagasaki, on the slave ships from Africa, in the arena at Rome. They were innocent of their suffering, we are guilty of complicity with ours; they had no choice in theirs, we bear responsibility for ours.

Created suffering, except where precluded by imposed pain, affects us all. The well-adjusted lie: listen to them at your risk; listen to them long enough, declaiming the official view, being serious with their slogans, and you lose contact with your own heart. Poets tell the truth: the sadness of Greece and Gethsemane, of Sodom and Gomorrah, of the Pharaohs and their minions and their slaves was as our own. It's part of being human, we differ from one another only in more or less. A few tranquil ones, with little conflict, suffer less; at the other extreme, stretched by despair to some dreadful cracking point, one goes berserk. In between are the rest of us, not miserable enough to go mad or jump off the bridge, yet never able if we are honest to say that we have come to terms with life, are at peace with ourselves, that we are happy.

The older I get the less I know, the darker the well of time. The enigma grows more bleak. I seek. I am concerned with suffering and with change, and I write equally for patient and therapist. What one should know will be useful, also, to the other. Here psychotherapy parts company with medicine.

The book for the surgeon is not the book for the surgical

patient. One delivers one's ailing body—with its abscess or tumor or broken bone—into the hands of the surgeon, and his most elementary information and skill will transcend anything the patient need know. The patient must cooperate—one green capsule three times a day, keep the leg elevated, force fluids—but need not understand how or why. The responsibility lies with the surgeon, the problem is his, his the accountability for failure, the credit for success. Patient and surgeon do not learn from the same text.

Many patients go to psychiatrists as if to surgeons, and many psychiatrists regard themselves as psychic surgeons. When such a patient comes to such a therapist a relationship of considerable length may result, but little else. For the job can be done, if at all, only by the patient. To assign this task to anyone else, however insightful or charismatic, is to disavow the source of change. In the process of personality change the role of the psychiatrist is catalytic. As a cause he is sometimes necessary, never sufficient. The responsibility of the patient does not end with free associating, with being on time, with keeping at it, paying his bills, or any other element of cooperation. He is accountable only to himself and this accountability extends all the way to the change which is desired, the achieving of it or the giving up on it.

So—consider one who suffers. Perhaps a woman with a warm heart but frigid. What can she do? Perhaps a mother who wants to love her children but does not. Maybe a homosexual living an endless series of hostile transient encounters. Perhaps a man in his middle fifties with a depressive character, normal to his friends, but constantly brushing away cobweb thoughts of suicide, one who is bored, finds no meaning in life, is ashamed. Consider one who suffers—anyone you know well. Consider perhaps yourself.

II

ACTION

I LIVE in a desert. Hour by hour feel myself dying. Surely I believe in something. Not much perhaps, but a little. What?

We are what we do. . . . Identity is the integration of behavior. If a man claims to be honest, we take him at his word. But if it should transpire that over the years he has been embezzling, we unhesitatingly discard the identity he adopts in words and ascribe to him the identity defined by his acts. "He claims to be honest," we say, "but he's really a thief."

One theft, however, does not make a thief. One act of forthrightness does not establish frankness; one tormenting of a cat does not make a sadist, nor one rescue of a fledgling, a savior. Action which defines a man, describes his character, is action which has been repeated over and over and so has come in time to be a coherent and relatively independent mode of behavior. At first it may have been fumbling and uncertain, may have required attention, effort, will—as when one first drives a car, first makes love, first robs a bank, first stands up against injustice. If one perseveres on any such course it comes in time to require less effort, less attention, begins to function smoothly; its small component behaviors become integrated within a larger pattern which has an ongoing dynamism and cohesiveness, carries its own authority. Such a mode then pervades the entire person, permeates other modes, colors other qualities, in some sense is living and operative even when the action is not being performed, or even considered. A young man who learns to drive a car thinks differently thereby, feels differently; when he meets a pretty girl who lives fifty miles away, the encounter carries implications he could not have felt as a bus rider. We may say, then, that he not only drives a car but has *become* a driver. If the action is shoplifting, we say not only that he steals from stores but that he has *become* a shoplifter.

Such a mode of action tends to maintain itself, to resist change. A thief is one who steals; stealing extends and reinforces the identity of thief, which generates further thefts, which further strengthen and deepen the identity. So long as one lives, change is possible; but the longer such behavior is continued the more force and authority it acquires, the more it permeates other consonant modes, subordinates other conflicting modes; changing back becomes steadily more difficult; settling down to an honest job, living on one's earnings becomes ever more unlikely. And what is said here of stealing applies equally to courage, cowardice, creativity, gambling, homosexuality, alcoholism, depression, or any other of the myriad ways of behaving, and hence of being. Identity is comprised of all such modes as may characterize a person, existing in varying degrees of integration and conflict. The greater the conflict the more unstable the identity; the more harmonious the various modes the more durable the identity.

The identity defined by action is present and past; it may also foretell the future, but not necessarily. Sometimes we act covertly, the eye does not notice the hand under the table, we construe the bribe to have been a gift, the running away to have been prudence, and so conceal from ourselves what we are. Then one day, perhaps, we drop the pretense, the illusion cracks. We have then the sense of an identity that has existed all along, and in some sense we knew it but would not let ourselves know that we knew it, but now we do, and in a blaze of candor say, "My God! I really am a crook!" or "I really am a coward!" We may then go too far and conclude that this identity is our "nature," that it was writ in the stars or in the double helix, that it transcends experience, that our actual lives have been the fulfilling of a preexisting pattern.

In fact it was writ only in our past choices. We are wise to believe it difficult to change, to recognize that character has a forward propulsion which tends to carry it unaltered into the future, but we need not believe it impossible to change. Our present and future choices may take us upon different courses which will in time comprise a different identity. It happens, sometimes, that the crook reforms, that the coward stands to fight.

. . . *and may do what we choose.* The identity defined by action is not, therefore, the whole person. Within us lies the potentiality for change, the freedom to choose other courses. When we admit that those "gifts" were bribes and say, "Well, then, I'm a crook," we have stated a fact, not a destiny; if we then invoke the leopard that can't change his spots, saying, "That's just the way I am, might as well accept it," we abandon the freedom to change and exploit what we have been in the past to avoid responsibility for what we shall be in the future.

Often we do not choose, but drift into those modes which eventually define us. Circumstances push and we yield. We did not choose to be what we have become, but gradually, imperceptibly became what we are by drifting into the doing of those things we now characteristically do. Freedom is not an objective attribute of life; alternatives without awareness yield no leeway. I open the door of my car and notice in a corner of vision an ant scurrying about on the smooth barren surface of the concrete parking lot, doomed momentarily to be crushed by one of the thousand passing wheels. There exists, however, a brilliant alternative for this gravely endangered creature: in a few minutes a woman will appear with a picnic basket and she and I will drive to a sunny hilltop meadow. This desperate ant has but to climb the wheel of my car to some sheltered ledge and in a half hour will be in a paradise for ants. But this option, unknown, unknowable, yields no freedom to the ant, who is doomed; and the only irony belongs to me who observes, who reflects that options potentially as meaningful to me as this one to this ant may at this moment be eluding *my* awareness; so I too may be doomed —this planet looks more like a parking lot every day.

Nothing guarantees freedom. It may never be achieved,

or having been achieved may be lost. Alternatives go unnoticed; foreseeable consequences are not foreseen; we may not know what we have been, what we are, or what we are becoming. We are the bearers of consciousness but of not very much, may proceed through a whole life without awareness of that which would have meant the most, the freedom which has to be noticed to be real. Freedom is the awareness of alternatives and of the ability to choose. It is contingent upon consciousness, and so may be gained or lost, extended or diminished.

Modern psychiatry found its image in the course of dealing with symptoms experienced as alien. A patient so afflicted seeks no alteration of character or personality, would be offended if the physician suggested such or pretended to any competence in that area. Nothing is felt to be wrong with the patient as a person, his self is not presented for examination or treatment. He is a patient only because he's sick, and his sickness consists of an ailment of which he wishes to be relieved. If the trouble is of recent onset and condenses a specific conflict of impulse and inhibition the medical model may be tenable: insight may function as medicine and dispel the symptom. On those exceedingly rare occasions when we still see such a case, we can be real doctors again and cure someone. The following is an example.

A thirty-five-year-old woman suddenly, and for the first time in her life, develops a spasm of the right foot and a left-sided migraine. Brain tumor is suspected but neurological examination is normal. On psychiatric consultation it is learned that she has been married fifteen years, has no children, is devoutly religious, cannot tolerate hostile feelings, but in fact despises her alcoholic husband. At a party, on the evening before her trouble began, she went upstairs looking for a bathroom and chanced upon her husband with a woman on his lap, the two of them in deep, prolonged kissing. She watched for a few moments, then backed away without being seen. On leaving the party, as her husband was drunk, she drove the car. Reaching home he stumbled out to open the garage door and for a moment was caught in the headlights. Just beyond him was a concrete wall. The motor was idling fast. She felt dizzy, passed a hand over her face. Upstairs, a few minutes later, her right foot began to twitch; during the night she woke with a headache.

In this case, after certain preparations, the interpretation, "You wanted to kill your husband," may effect a cure. No will is necessary, no action, no change in being. Insight is enough.

Most psychiatrists know such cases only from reading examples like this one. The patients who actually appear in their offices—whatever their symptoms—suffer problems of being. When the symptom is migraine it has occurred not once but hundreds of times, over many years. It is not the expression of a specific conflict, but a response to any conflict, any tension, a way of running from whatever seems too much; it has become a mode of being in the world. The patient may feel it as alien, want to be rid of it, but it has become useful in a thousand unnoticed ways; its removal would not be simple relief but would expose the patient to conflicts which he has no other way of handling. The symptom does not afflict the patient, it *is* the patient.

This headache will not dissolve with insight, and here the medical model breaks down. What is called for is not cure of illness but change in what one is. Insight is not enough. Effort and will are crucial.

The most common illusion of patients and, strangely, even of experienced therapists, is that insight produces change; and the most common disappointment of therapy is that it does not. Insight is instrumental to change, often an essential part of the process, but does not directly achieve it. The most comprehensive and penetrating interpretation—true, relevant, well expressed, perfectly timed—may lie inert in the patient's mind; for he may always, if he be so inclined, say, "Yes, but it doesn't help." If a therapist takes the position, as many do, that a correct interpretation is one that gets results, that the getting of results is an essential criterion for the correctness of an interpretation, he will be driven to more and more remote reconstructions of childhood events, will move further and further from present reality, responding always to the patient's "Yes, but why?" with further reachings for more distant antecedents. The patient will be saying, in effect, "Yes, but what are you going to do about it?" and the therapist, instead of saying, as he should, "What are *you* going to do about it?" responds according to his professional overestimate of the efficacy of insight by struggling toward some ever more basic formulation. Some patients don't want to change, and when a therapist takes on the task of changing such a one he assumes a contest which the patient always wins. The magic of insight, of unconscious psychodynamics, proves no magic at all; the most marvelous interpretation falls useless—like a gold spoon from the hand of a petulant child who doesn't want his spinach.

An anguished woman enters our office, sits down, weeps, begins to talk, and we listen. We are supposed to know what's up here, what the problem *really* is, and what to do about it. But the theories with which we have mapped the soul don't help, the life she relates is unlike any other. We may nevertheless cling to our map, telling ourselves we know where we are and all is well, but if we look up into the jungle of her misery we know we are lost. And what have we to go on? What to cling to? That people may change, that one person can help another. That's all. Maybe that's enough.

The suffering is a given, but the problem is a choice, is subjective and arbitrary, rests finally upon nothing more than the patient's will, upon his being able to say "This . . . is what I want to change."

Those psychiatrists who regard themselves in the manner of medical men would disagree, would hold that a psychic problem—homosexuality, for example, or compulsivity—is objectively verifiable, that a panel of competent therapists would concur. This view would hold that the problem "emerges" from the "material," is recognized and defined by the therapist who then presents it to the patient along with his recommendation for treatment.

But since a problem is something for which a solution is sought, only the patient can designate it. The therapist may perceive that a certain conflict leads regularly to such and such situations which cause suffering. But a cause of suffering is not a problem unless it is taken as such by the patient.

Likewise the goal of treatment must be determined by the patient. The only appropriate goal for the therapist is to assist. If the therapist cannot in good faith help to the end desired he is free to decline, but he cannot reasonably work toward goals of his own choosing. Even so benign a therapeutic aim as to "help the patient realize his potentials" may be too much. It is too much if that is not what the patient wants. Sometimes, indeed, the patient may want the opposite, may feel that the trouble comes from his having begun to realize incompatible potentialities, and that from some of these he now must turn away.

III

FREEDOM
AND
NECESSITY

FREEDOM is that range of experience wherein events, courses of action, attitudes, decisions, accommodations are seen as elective. It may be more or less, so we need ask how much we want. In small things we always want choice. What color to paint the house? buy an Olds or a Buick? go to the Bergman film or the Ozawa concert? It would be onerous to be constrained here. In deeper matters we want to be held back. We might choose to live or die, but prefer *not* to choose, want to believe rather that we *have* to live. A kind man does not ponder becoming a sadist, an honest man does not consider whether to become a bandit; we prefer to have such matters settled, removed from choice and hence from freedom.

In between such minor and major issues lies the middle ground of decision and action wherein some find freedom and choice while others find constraint and necessity. One man sees himself inextricably stuck in a marriage, a career, in obligations to children, relatives, colleagues, bound to his way and place of life, unable to change. Another in the same circumstances finds it possible to resign as judge of the circuit court, divorce a Philadelphia Mainline wife after twenty-four years of marriage and three children, move to Italy, live with an actress, take up painting. If we forgo the moral condemnation we generally visit upon those of greater scope and daring than ourselves we are likely to discover great envy.

Necessity is that range of experience wherein events, courses of action, attitudes, decisions are seen as determined by forces outside ourselves which we cannot alter. A bored woman says, "I'd like to take a job, but can't leave home because of the children." With that "can't" she alleges necessity: staying home or leaving home is not open, the decision is imposed, runs counter to her wants; she designates her children's needs as her necessity. Her prerogative to do this is clear, is granted, but it must be noted that nothing external to herself requires this view. Certainly her children's needs do not require it: within the same block other mothers manage somehow with baby-sitters and so hold jobs. The necessity that constrains her does not constrain them; it is of a different order than that which would derive from locked doors and barred windows.

The realm of necessity, therefore, must comprise two categories: the subjective or arbitrary, and the objective or mandatory. Mandatory necessity—like natural law which cannot be disobeyed—is that which cannot be suspended. It derives from forces, conditions, events which lie beyond the self, not subject to choice, unyielding to will and effort. "I wish I had blue eyes," ". . . wish I were twenty again," ". . . wish I could fly," ". . . wish I lived in the court of the Sun King." Such wishes are futile, choice is inoperative; the necessity impartially constrains. And since it cannot be put aside there's not much arguing about it. "If you jump you will fall—whether or not you choose to fly." There is consensus, we don't dwell on it, we accept.

Arbitrary necessity derives from forces within the personality, but construed to be outside. The force may be either impulse or prohibition: "I didn't want to drink, but couldn't help it." That is to say, the impulse to drink does not lie within the "I." The "I," which is of course the locus of choice, does not "want" to drink, would choose otherwise, but is overwhelmed by alien force. "I want to marry you," a woman says to her lover, "want it more than anything in the world. But I can't divorce my husband. He couldn't take it . . . would break down. He depends on me. It would kill him." Here it is loyalty, caring for another's welfare, which is alleged to lie outside the deciding "I," which therefore cannot choose, cannot do what it "wants," but is held to an alien course. As though she were saying, "I do not here preside over internal conflict, do not listen to contending claims within myself to arrive finally at an anguished, fallible decision, but am coerced by a mandate beyond my jurisdiction. I yield to necessity." The issue is not one of conscious versus unconscious. The contending forces are both conscious. The issue is the boundary of the self, the limits of the "I."

Arbitrary necessity, therefore—like man-made law—is that which may be suspended, disobeyed. When dealing with ourselves the constraining force seems inviolable, a solid wall before us, as though we really "can't," have no choice; and if we say so often enough, long enough, and mean it, we may make it so. But when we then look about and observe others doing what we "can't" do we must conclude that the constraining force is not an attribute of the environing world, not the way things are, but a mandate from within ourselves which we, strangely, exclude from the "I."

The lady who "wants" to marry her lover but "can't" divorce her husband might here object. "When I said 'can't,'" she might say, "it was just a way of speaking, a metaphor. It meant that staying with my husband represents duty, not desire, that's all. In a theoretical way I could choose . . . I know that. But it's just theoretical. Because . . . you see, the conflict is so terribly unequal, the considerations that make me stay, that absolutely demand I stay with my husband . . . they're so overwhelmingly strong, there's really no choice. That's all I mean."

We make serious record of her objection. In passing we note with surprise that the inequality of the conflict leads her to conclude there is "really no choice," whereas this same circumstance would have led us to say rather that the choice is easy, one she might arrive at promptly, with the conviction of being right.

It's only a metaphor, she says. In some theoretical way, she says, she is aware of choice. Perhaps. But we have doubt. In any event we must point out that she specifically denies this choice for which she now claims oblique awareness, that she locates the determining duty outside the "I" and its "wants." And we might add that if she continues such metaphorical speech long enough she will eventually convince even herself; her "theoretical" choice will become more and more theoretical until, with no remaining consciousness of option, it will disappear in thin air. She then will have made actual something that may once have been but a metaphor. Nothing guarantees our freedom. Deny it often enough and one day it will be gone, and we'll not know how or when.

Objective necessity is not arguable. My lover dies, I weep, beat my fists on the coffin. Everyone knows what I want; everyone knows that nothing will avail, no prayer, no curse, no desperate effort, nothing, that I shall never get her back. When there is argument about necessity, the alleged constraint is arbitrary, subjective. A house in flames, a trapped child, a restraining neighbor: "You can't go in! It's hopeless." I see it differently: I *can* go in—if I have the nerve. There may be a chance. It's not clear whether the situation permits or proscribes; the difference of opinion indicates that the necessity at issue is arbitrary. My neighbor's statement is more plea than observation; he asks me to perceive that the contemplated action is precluded, to "see" that there is no choice. By so deciding I can make it so. If I agree it is impossible, then—even if mistaken—my having arrived at that judgment will, in a matter of moments, make it true. Our judgments fall within the field of events being judged, so themselves become events, and so alter the field. We survey the course of history and conclude, "Wars are inevitable." The judgment seems detached, as if we observed from a distant galaxy; in fact it comes from within and, like all judgments, it may be mistaken. It is not inert, it has consequences, shapes action, moves interest and behavior from, for example, the politics of dissent to the connoisseurship of wine; and so chips off one more fragment of the obstacle to war, thereby makes more likely the war which, when it comes, will vindicate our original judgment and the behavior which issued from it. So we create the necessity which then constrains us, constrains ever more tightly day after day, so vindicating ever more certainly our wisdom in having perceived from the outset we were not free. Finally we are bound hand and foot and may exclaim triumphantly, how right we were!

The areas of necessity and of freedom vary in proportion to each other and in absolute measure. They vary, also, from person to person, and, within the same person, from time to time. Together they comprise the total extent of available experience the range of which is a function of awareness and concern.

Adolescence, traditionally, is the time of greatest freedom, the major choices thereafter being progressively made, settled, and buried, one after another, never to be reopened. These days, however, an exhumation of such issues in later life has become quite common, with a corresponding increase in freedom which makes life again as hazardous as in youth.

Throughout our lives the proportion of necessity to freedom depends upon our tolerance of conflict: the greater our tolerance the more freedom we retain, the less our tolerance the more we jettison; for high among the uses of necessity is relief from tension. What we can't alter we don't have to worry about; so the enlargement of necessity is a measure of economy in psychic housekeeping. The more issues we have closed the fewer we have to fret about. For many of us, for example, the issues of stealing and of homosexuality are so completely buried that we no longer have consciousness of option, and so no longer in these matters have freedom. We may then walk through Tiffany's or go to the ballet without temptation or conflict, whereas for one to whom these are still live issues, the choice depending upon a constantly shifting balance of fallibly estimated rewards of gain or pleasure as against risks of capture or shame, such jaunts may entail great tension.

Tranquillity, however, has risks of its own. As we expand necessity and so relieve ourselves of conflict and responsibility, we are relieved, also, in the same measure, of authority and significance. When there arises then a crisis which does not fall within our limited routine we are frightened, without resources, insignificant.

For some people necessity expands cancerously, every possibility of invention and variation being transformed into inflexible routine until all of freedom is eaten away. The extreme in psychic economy is an existence in which everything occurs by law. Since life means conflict, such a state is living death. When, in the other direction, the area of necessity is too much diminished we become confused, anxious, may be paralyzed by conflict, may reach eventually the extreme of panic.

The more we are threatened, fragile, vulnerable, the more we renounce freedom in favor of an expanding necessity. Observing others then who laugh at risk, who venture on paths from which we have turned back, we feel envy; they are courageous where we are timid. We come close to despising ourselves, but recover quickly, can always take refuge in a hidden determinism. "It's all an illusion," we say; "it looks like their will and daring as against my inhibition and weakness, but that *must* be illusion. Because life is lawful. Nothing happens by chance. Not a single atom veers off course at random. My inhibition is not a failure of nerve. We can't see the forces that mold us, but they are there. The genetic and experiential dice are loaded with factors unknown, unknowable, not of our intending, are thrown in circumstances over which we have no vision or control; we are stuck with the numbers that turn up. Beware the man who claims to be captain of his soul, he's first mate at the very best."

The more we are strong and daring the more we will diminish necessity in favor of an expanding freedom. "We are responsible," we say, "for what we are. We create ourselves. We have done as we have chosen to do, and by so doing have become what we are. If we don't like it, tomorrow is another day, and we may do differently."

Each speaks truly for himself, the one is just so determined, the other is just so free; but each overstates his truth in ascribing his constraint or his liberty to life at large. These truths are partial, do not contend with each other. Each expresses a quality of experience. Which view one chooses to express, to the exclusion of the other, better describes the speaker than the human condition.

In every situation, for every person, there is a realm of freedom and a realm of constraint. One may live in either realm. One must recognize the irresistible forces, the iron fist, the stone wall—must know them for what they are in order not to fall into the sea like Icarus—but, knowing them, one may turn away and live in the realm of one's freedom. A farmer must know the fence which bounds his land but need not spend his life standing there, looking out, beating his fists on the rails; better he till his soil, think of what to grow, where to plant the fruit trees. However small the area of freedom, attention and devotion may expand it to occupy the whole of life.

Look at the wretched people huddled in line for the gas chambers at Auschwitz. If they do anything other than move on quietly, they will be clubbed down. Where is freedom? . . . But wait. Go back in time, enter the actual event, the very moment: they are thin and weak, and they smell; hear the weary shuffling steps, the anguished catch of breath, the clutch of hand. Enter now the mind of one hunched and limping man. The line moves slowly; a few yards ahead begin the steps down. He sees the sign, someone whispers "showers," but he knows what happens here. He is struggling with a choice: to shout "Comrades! They will kill you! Run!" or to say nothing. This option, in the few moments remaining, is his whole life. If he shouts he dies now, painfully; if he moves on silently he dies but minutes later. Looking back on him in time and memory, we find the moment poignant but the freedom negligible. It makes no difference, we think, in that situation, his election of daring or of inhibition. Both are futile, without consequence. History sees no freedom for him, notes only constraint, labels him victim. But in the consciousness of

31

that one man it makes great difference whether or not he experience the choice. For if he knows the constraint and nothing else, if he thinks "Nothing is possible," then he is living his necessity; but if, perceiving the constraint, he turns from it to a choice between two possible courses of action, then—however he choose—he is living his freedom. This commitment to freedom may extend to the last breath.

IV

STEEL
FINGERS

THERE is a point of view which holds that freedom is an illusion. Freedom is central to our traditional view of man, writes B. F. Skinner, and we feel comfortable with it, but the scientific study of behavior has shown it to be a fiction. "Personal exemption from a complete determinism is revoked as a scientific analysis progresses, particularly in accounting for the behavior of the individual."[1] "In the traditional picture a person perceives the world around him, selects features to be perceived, discriminates among them, judges them good or bad, changes them to make them better (or, if he is careless, worse), and may be held responsible for his action and justly rewarded or punished for its consequences. In the scientific picture a person is a member of a species shaped by evolutionary contingencies of survival, displaying behavioral processes which bring him under the control of the environment in which he lives. . . . The direction of the controlling relation is reversed: A person

1. B. F. Skinner, *Beyond Freedom and Dignity* (New York: Alfred A. Knopf, 1971), p. 21.

does not act upon the world, the world acts upon him."[2]

Let us give this view the benefit of a generous doubt, not being put off by the arrogance with which science is claimed for but one side of the argument. Let us take, indeed, the position of a determinist and argue Skinner's case with more force and less jargon. What shall we say, then, of the alleged freedom of that Jew limping his last few steps at Auschwitz?

It is true he could cry out or remain silent. True, that is, so far as an observer can ascertain. His reality, which permits him but a few moments more to live, permits both. It is true, further, that he feels freedom and struggles with choice, true that in doing the one or the other he will believe himself the author of the action and hence responsible. All this the determinist may admit as primary data of experience, known by introspection to each of us in the innumerable decisions of everyday life. But this felt freedom, the determinist asserts, measures only the degree to which the shaping causes lie outside awareness. For though the outer reality in which our victim is fatally enmeshed and of which he is so acutely aware permits both actions, there is an inner reality which permits but one. This inner reality has been shaped by all the circumstances of his life, circumstances now beyond his awareness, remote from his present experience, which have molded him into the man he is and so have brought it about that he perceives these options, struggles with this choice, and has long since foreclosed the issue of which course he

2. *Ibid.*, p. 211.

will choose. We are lived, says Groddeck, by unknown and unknowable forces.

Where shall we seek the nature of man? In the stars? In the earth? In the snarl of the tiger, the terror of the heart? I seek within.

I sit in a leather chair and listen to patients, watch their eyes and hands and mouths, peer into their lives, reveal nothing of my own. It is quiet in this room; words and weeping are subdued. When the patients have gone it becomes utterly still. I sit here and write. The phone does not ring.

My life is solitude. I *want* it so. Had I no choice, my wanting it so might be construed as making the best of something unavoidable: the disdain of a starving man for unavailable food must be discounted. My preference, however, need not be discounted, for I have choice. Invitations arrive in the mail—to lecture, to appear on television, to be interviewed, to debate, to participate in symposia. "I very much appreciate your kind invitation," I reply, "and regret that I must decline. I am engaged in a work which I do not feel free to interrupt. . . ."

The determinist is not convinced. "Oh I take your word for what you feel," he says, "I believe you. You *want* it this way. I am concerned, however, to discover what it is that *determines* what you want. You look lonely. Your face is starved and haunted. People want to feed you. There's no pleasure in your life so far as I can see; it's all work. The phone does not ring and you *want* it this way. How curious! How very much in need of explanation! You

would have me see it as a manifestation of unfettered preference, arbitrary, uncaused, like the spinning of a compass
needle in a world without poles. I can't believe it. What
you want is tendentious, is reliable, is fixed, a compass
needle that points true north to some hidden lodestone
of conditioning experience. People know you won't come
out. I cannot see into your life, but you are a psychoanalyst, you must know about these things. What is that
lodestone? Sniff it out. Dig. Search with that kind of
patient cunning that insinuates itself behind proud asserta-
tions. Listen for stifled voices within, and eventually you
will discover that what you so independently *want* follows
from your past like an arrow from the bow." Anxiety ac-
quired when one is a child, writes Skinner and, equally,
writes Freud, survives into old age.

It is late at night. I feel a strange unease. The room is
so quiet the hum of a clock is the roar of a distant ocean,
a tide of people and events washing on other shores, passing me by. I feel unworthy, remember times when I have
been angry with this or that person. How strange! I cannot
now imagine being angry at anyone. I feel undeserving,
I should be grateful just to be alive, overwhelmed if anyone should like me, if a patient should find me helpful,
am dismayed to recall moments of intolerance, of critical-
ness. Who am I to set standards of conduct, to pass judgment on anyone?

Suddenly I cannot bear the silence. I put a record on
the phonograph. A Mahler song:

> I have become lost to the world . . .
> So long has it heard nothing of me
> It may well believe me dead.

I say good night to my last patient, enter the elevator. It is a tiny, brightly lighted cubicle with a shelf and a telephone, just large enough for one person. It ascends slowly in a tall house, makes a throbbing hum. I am tired and relaxed. The phone rings; it is my friend Ellery Quiven, a psychoanalyst. After an exchange of amenities he says, "A Mrs. Foster called me today, said you had referred her. I wonder if you would tell me about her." She is a woman I saw in consultation a few days ago, I remember her well. As I begin to describe her, steel fingers seize my heart. My chest constricts as if in a giant hand. I struggle to breathe, to continue talking. My sentences break down. Ellery helps out by beginning himself to talk. I am profoundly humiliated by his kindness, struggle on to a premature conclusion. The elevator has stopped at the top floor. I hang up the phone which is dripping wet in my clenched fist.

We sit at ease with our old friends the Emersons, drink sherry, chat. My wife is reminded of a passage in a book I have just written which makes use of something the Emersons once told us. "Oh read it to them!" she exclaims. "They'd love it." I'm pleased, for it is a passage of remarkable imagery and rhythm; I want to read it. I go to get the book and, returning, feel again the steel fingers, the hand closing around my chest. Heart leaps like a desperate fish. "*You* read it," I say, and give the book to my wife. As she reads, my anxiety subsides.

Fourteen guests sit at an oval table in our circular dining room. White damask cloth, flowers, crystal, gleam of silver, faces illumined by the glow of candles. The edges of the room are in darkness, shadows move on the high ceiling. Lace curtains hang softly over three sets of tall French doors, beyond them a terrace bright in moonlight, an iron gate. The food is excellent, the wine old and rare; there is a pleasant hum of voices.

The lady on my left is silent. Trying to think of something to entertain her, my eyes rest on the iron gate at the end of the terrace. "A most unusual thing happened a few nights ago," I say to her. "I was downstairs in my study, writing. It was ten o'clock. The phone rings. I pick it up, and for a few moments there is no one on the line. I hear the sound of a typewriter, a radio, someone talking. It sounds like an office. Then a man comes on the line. He knows my name. He seems to read, as if from a scrap of paper, my address, and I confirm it. It begins to seem very curious. 'Well . . .' he says hesitantly, 'is everybody all right at your place?' 'Who are you?' I say. 'This is Mission Emergency Hospital. We got a call here from a lady who said people are dying at your place, said we should send an ambulance right away. Is everybody all right?' Upstairs I hear my daughter playing the oboe. I assure him we are well. 'She sounded like a crackpot all right,' he says, 'but thought I'd better check it out. She said we should come prepared to break down the door, that we shouldn't hesitate because people are dying inside. Said she would meet us there.' "

Suddenly I become aware that the table has fallen silent; everyone is looking at me, listening. "I came upstairs then," I continue; "everything seemed normal. I looked out on that terrace. The lights were off, there was no moon, it was absolute darkness. I was standing there, by that door, wondering, when I heard the sound of rapid footsteps coming up the outside stairway. I marveled that anyone could come so fast in such blackness. I looked out through these curtains, expecting perhaps to see a flashlight, but nothing. Then the iron gate began to rattle. Someone was shaking it. It quickly became more violent. Whoever it was was meaning to break it down. I switched on the outside lights, opened the door and went out. The noise stopped. A slender well-dressed woman was standing at the gate. About forty, I would say. As I approached she dropped her hand from the gate, shrank back in horror. 'Good evening,' I said. She raised a hand as if to ward off something. Her face was ashen. After a moment, in a tense whisper, she said, 'Are you all right?' 'Yes, I'm all right. Why do you ask?' Slowly she looked me up and down. She looked particularly at my wrists, as if to see blood run down my arm, drip from my fingers. She looked at my feet, then back at my face, all with an expression of shocked disbelief. Finally, as if reluctantly accepting the evidence of her eyes, she again whispered, 'And the others inside?' 'Everyone's all right,' I said. She looked up at the house in horror, looked at the windows, the roof, yet was further shaken in her conviction, I think, by the sound of scales being played on the oboe. The dog wandered out wagging his tail. 'Who *are* you?' I said. She shook her head desperately, stepped back. I moved forward, opened the gate. 'What is your name?' I said. She turned, fled down the steps. A taxi was waiting in front, motor running, door open."

Everyone is fascinated by the strange story, everyone

discusses it. We are impressed by the powerful and mysteri-
ous force that drove this poor woman out of her house and
across town to a strange house and up all those stairs in
darkness, prepared to break down a door to find the car-
nage her mind had created. And something else is fascinat-
ing here, something my guests could not know: in telling
this story, in seeing their eyes fixed on me, feeling their
rapt attention, I felt no anxiety. Where were the steel
fingers? How did I escape them?

I discern a pattern. The trigger for anxiety is the giving
of an account upon which I may be judged. In the elevator
I felt like a student psychiatrist presenting a case to a senior
colleague. In preparing to read the passage from my book
I felt like a student writer who is called upon to read his
work before a class. Steel fingers hinge on primitive dis-
tinctions; for so soon as it was my wife who was reading,
it no longer seemed that it was *I* who was being judged,
but the passage as such. I was removed from judgment
and so from danger. Likewise, in telling the story of the
mad woman, I must have been calmed by my perception
that our guests were interested in the story, not in its telling, that they were trying to arrive at a judgment of the
woman being described, not of him who described her.

The occasion for anxiety, therefore, is any situation
which has somewhat the form of my giving an account of
myself. I must infer within me a hidden conviction that
my accounting will be inadequate, that the judgment will
be adverse and beyond appeal. I must infer, further, a
conviction that the adverse judgment will be binding upon

my own view, that I will be unable to retain even a private judgment of myself as adequate or innocent. As a computer is programmed to react in a certain way, so I have been programmed to react in this way. Something imprinted on my character in childhood holds me, year after year, decade after decade, faithfully to the same course.

I know when it happened. I remember that long summer.

V

GRASS

I T WAS the last day of school.
The report cards had been distributed, and—to my great
relief—I had passed. Now at eleven o'clock in the morning
I was on my way home with two friends. We felt ex-
hilaration at the prospect of three months of freedom and
manifested it by pushing each other, yelling, throwing
rocks at a bottle, chasing a grass snake, and rolling a log
into the creek. Being eight years old, it took us a long time
to reach our homes. Before parting we made plans to meet
that afternoon to play ball. I ran through the tall grass up
to the back door and into the kitchen. My mother was
stirring something on the stove.

"Mama, I passed!"

"Not so loud, hon." She leaned over and kissed me, then
looked at the report card. "This is very good. Show it to
Daddy if he's not asleep."

I went through the bedroom to the glassed-in porch
where my father lay sick with tuberculosis. The bed faced
away from the door and I could not tell whether he was
asleep or not.

"Daddy?"

"Come in, son."

"I passed," I said, offering the card.

He smiled and I lowered my eyes. I could never bring myself to face for long the level gaze of those pale blue eyes which seemed effortlessly to read my mind. He looked over the report. "I see you got seventy-five in conduct."

"Yes, sir."

"Do you have an explanation?"

"No, sir."

"Do you think you deserved a better grade?"

"No . . . sir."

"Then you *do* have an explanation?"

I twisted one foot around the other. "Yes, sir. I guess so, sir."

"What is the explanation?"

This tireless interrogation could, I knew, be carried on for hours. Mumbling the words, I began to recount my sins. "I guess I . . . talked too much."

"Speak up, son."

"Yes, sir. I talked too much . . . and laughed . . . and cut up."

"Do you find silence so difficult?"

"Sir?"

"Was it so hard to be quiet?"

"Yes . . . sir. I guess so."

"You don't seem to find it difficult now."

I looked up and found him smiling. It wasn't going to be so bad after all. "But the other grades are good," he said. I grinned and turned to look out the window. Heat waves shimmered over the tin roof of the barn; away to

the west was an unbroken field of sunflowers. Everything
was bathed in, and seemed to be made drowsy by, the hot,
bright sunlight. I thought of playing ball and wished dinner
were over so I could go now. "Daddy, can I go over to
Paul's house after dinner?" Almost before the words were
out I realized my mistake. I should have asked my mother
first. She might have said yes without consulting my
father.

"No. You have to work, son."

"What've I got to do?"

He looked out over the several acres which we called
the back yard. "You have to cut the grass."

Through a long wet spring the grass had sprung up
until it was nearly a foot high. Now, in June, the rain was
over and the heat was beginning to turn the grass brown.
As we had no lawn mower, any cutting of grass or weeds
was done by hoe, scythe, or sickle. It was with one of
these I assumed the grass would be cut, but I was mistaken. After dinner my father gave me directions. The tool
was to be an old, ivory-handled, straight-edge razor. The
method was to grasp a handful of grass in the left hand
and cut it level with the ground with the razor. The grass
was to be put in a basket, along with any rocks or sticks
that might be found on the ground. When the basket was
full it was to be removed some hundred yards where the
grass could be emptied and burned. When the razor was
dull it was to be sharpened on a whetstone in the barn.

I changed my clothes, put on a straw hat, and went to
work. Unable to realize the extent of the task or to gauge
the time required, my only thought was to finish as soon

as possible so as to be able to play before the afternoon was over. I began in the center of the yard and could see my father watching from his bed on the porch. After a few experimental slashes an idea occurred to me. I walked to the house and stood under the windows of the porch.

"Daddy."

"Yes, son."

"When I've finished can I play baseball?"

"Yes."

I resumed work, thinking I would cut fast and get it over in a couple of hours. For a few minutes all went well; there was some satisfaction in watching the thin steel cut easily through dry grass. I grabbed big handfuls and hacked away with gusto. Soon my father called. Obediently I walked to the porch. "Yes, sir?" He was looking through field glasses at the small patch of ground that had been cleared.

"Son, I want you to cut the grass *level* with the ground. Therefore you will have to cut slower and more carefully. Take a smaller handful at a time so you can cut it evenly. Also, you must pick up every stone." This referred to the few pebbles left in the cleared area. "Do you understand?"

"Yes, sir."

"Now go back and do that patch over again, and cut it level with the ground."

"Yes, sir."

Walking back I wondered why I had not started in some part of the yard out of my father's view. The work was now harder; for the stubble was only one or two inches high and was difficult to hold while being cut. It took an hour to do again the area originally cleared in a few minutes. By this time I was tired and disheartened. Sweat ran down my forehead and into my eyes; my mouth was dry. The razor could not be held by the handle, for the blade would fold back. It had to be held by its narrow shank which already had raised a blister. Presently I heard my friends; soon they came into view and approached the fence.

"Whatya doin'?"

"Cuttin' the grass."

"What's that you're cuttin' it with?"

"A razor."

They laughed. "That's a funny thing to be cuttin' grass with."

"Son!" The boys stopped laughing and I went to the porch.

"Yes, sir?"

"If you want to talk to your friends, you may; but don't stop working while you talk."

"Yes, sir." I went back to the basket and resumed cutting.

"What'd he say?" Paul asked in a lowered voice.

"He said I had to work."

"You cain't play ball?"

"No."

"How long is he going to make you work?"

"I don't know."

"Well . . . I guess we might as well go on."

I looked up with longing. They were standing outside the fence, poking their toes idly through the palings. James was rhythmically pounding his fist into the socket of a first baseman's mitt.

"Yeah, let's get goin'."

"Can you get away later on?" Paul asked.

"Maybe I can. I'll try. I'll see if he'll let me." The two boys began to wander off. "I'll try to come later," I called urgently, hoping my father would not hear.

When they were gone I tried for a while to cut faster, but my hand hurt. Several times I had struck rocks with the razor, and the blade was getting dull. Gingerly I got up from my sore knees, went to the hydrant, allowed the water to run until cool, and drank from my cupped hands. Then I went to the barn and began whetting the blade on the stone. When it was sharp I sat down to rest. Being out of my father's sight I felt relatively secure for the moment. The chinaberry tree cast a liquid pattern of sun and shadow before the door. The berries were green and firm, just right for a slingshot.

"Son!"

With a sense of guilt I hurried to my father's window. "Yes, sir."

"Get back to work. It's not time to rest yet."

At midafternoon I looked about and saw how little I had done. Heat waves shimmered before my eyes and I realized that I would not finish today and perhaps not tomorrow. Leaving the razor on the ground, I made the familiar trek to my father's window.

"Daddy."

"Yes."

"Can I quit now?"

"No, son."

"I cain't finish it this afternoon."

"I know."

"Then cain't I go play ball now and finish it tomorrow?"

"No."

"When can I play ball?"

"When you have finished cutting the grass."

"How long do you think it'll take me?"

"Two or three months."

"Well, can . . . ?"

"Now that's enough. Go back to work."

I resumed work at a sullenly slow pace. To spare my knees I sat down, cutting around me as far as I could reach, then moving to a new place and sitting down again.

"Son!"

I went back to the porch. "Yes, sir."

"Do you want to be a lazy, no-account scoundrel?" The voice was harsh and angry.

"No, sir."

"Then don't you ever let me see you sitting down to work again! Now you get back there as quick as you can and stand on your knees."

The afternoon wore on with excruciating slowness. The sun gradually declined. The thin shank of the razor cut into my hand and the blisters broke. I showed them to my father, hoping they would prove incapacitating, but he bandaged them and sent me back. Near sundown I heard the sounds of my friends returning to their homes, but they did not come by to talk. Finally my mother came to the back door, said supper was ready. The day's work was over.

When I woke the next morning I thought it was another school day, then remembered the preceding afternoon and knew that school was far better than cutting grass. I knew that my father intended for me to continue the work, but as no specific order had been given for this particular day there was possibility of escape. I decided to ask my mother for permission to play and be gone before my father realized what had happened. My mother was cooking breakfast when I finished dressing. I made myself useful and waited until, for some reason, she went on the back porch. Now we were separated from my father by four rooms and clearly out of earshot.

"Mama, can I go over to Paul's house?"

"Why yes, hon, I guess so."

That was my mother. To the reasonable request she said yes immediately; the unreasonable required a varying amount of cajolery, but in the end that, too, would be granted. When breakfast was over, I quickly got my cap, whispered a soft good-bye, and started out. I had reached the back door when she called. "Be sure you come back before dinner."

"Son!"

I stopped. In another moment I would have been far enough away to pretend I had not heard. But though my conscience might be deaf to a small voice, it was not deaf to this sternly audible one. If I ran now I would never be able to look at my father and say, "No, I didn't hear you." I gave my mother a reproachful glance as I went back through the kitchen. "Now I won't get to go," I said darkly.

I entered the glass porch and stood by the bed, eyes lowered. I was aware of omitting the required "Yes, sir," but did not care.

"Where were you off to?"

"To Paul's."

"Who told you you could go?"

"Mama."

"Did you ask her?"

"Yes."

"Yes *what?*"

"Yes, sir," I said sulkily.

"Didn't you know I wanted you to work today?"

"No, sir."

"Don't you remember my telling you that you could not play until you finished cutting the grass?"

"No, sir." One lie followed another now. "Anyway . . . that will take just about . . . all summer." My mouth was dry and I was swallowing heavily. "James and Paul . . . don't have to work and . . . I don't see why . . . I . . . have to work all the time."

I choked, my eyes burned, and tears were just one harsh word away. After a moment I saw the covers of the bed move; my father's long, wasted legs appeared. The tears broke, flooding my face. My father stood up, slowly, with difficulty, found his slippers, and put on a bathrobe. My ear was seized and twisted by a bony hand, and I was propelled into the bathroom. My father sat on the edge of the tub and held me in front of him. The fingers were relentless, and it seemed that my ear would be torn from my head.

"Look at me, son."

Tears were dripping from my chin, and every other moment my chest was convulsed by a rattling inspiration.

Trying to stop crying, I managed at last to raise my head and look in my father's face. The head and neck were thin. The skin had a grayish glint, and the lines that ran down from his nose were straight. His eyes were steady, and on their level, searching gaze my conscience was impaled.

"Do you know why you are going to be punished?"

The pose of injured innocence was gone now. My guilt seemed everywhere, there was no place to hide.

"Yes . . . sir."

"Why?"

"Because . . . I . . . didn't tell the . . . truth." It was terrible to look into those eyes.

"And?" The question was clipped and hard.

"And . . . because . . . ."

I tried to search my conscience and enumerate my sins, but my mind was a shambles and my past was mountainous with guilt. I could not speak. My eyes dropped.

"Look at me, son."

It was agony to lift my eyes again to that knifelike gaze, that implacable accusation.

"You are being punished because you tried to get your mother's permission for an act you knew to be wrong. You were scoundrel enough to do that!" the razored voice said. "Do you understand?"

"Yes . . . sir."

"You are being punished, further, because you were sullen and insubordinate. Do you understand?"

"Yes . . . sir."

I saw the other hand move and felt the old, sick terror. The hand grasped the clothes of my back and lifted me onto my father's knees. My head hung down to the floor. The hand began to rise and fall.

"Do you understand why you're being punished?"

"Ye . . . es . . . sir."

The blows were heavy and I cried.

"Will you ever do any of those things again?"

"No . . . sir."

The whipping lasted about a minute, after which I was placed on my feet. "Now, stop crying and wash your face. Then go out in the yard to work."

Still sobbing, I approached the lavatory, turned on a trickle of water. Behind me I heard my father stand and slowly leave the room. I held both hands under the faucet, stared with unseeing eyes at the drops of water tumbling over my fingers. Gradually the sobs diminished. I washed my face and left the room, closing the door softly. Passing through the kitchen I was aware that my mother was looking at me with compassion, but I avoided her eyes. To look at her now would be to cry again.

All that day I worked steadily and quietly, asked no questions, made no requests. The work was an expiation and my father found no occasion to criticize. Several times my mother brought out something cold for me to drink. She did not mention my punishment but knowledge of it was eloquent in her eyes. In the afternoon I began to feel better and thought of my friends and of playing ball. Knowing it to be out of the question, I only dreamed about it.

That evening when supper was over and the dishes washed my father called me.

"Tell him you're sorry," my mother whispered.

In our house after every punishment there had to be a reconciliation, the integrity of the bonds that held us had to be reaffirmed. Words of understanding had to be spoken, tokens of love given and received. I walked out on the porch. The sky was filled with masses of purple and red.

"Do you feel better now, son?"

"Yes, sir." The blue eyes contained a reflection of the sunset. "I'm sorry I acted the way I did this morning."

A hand was laid on my head. "You said you didn't know why you had to work, didn't you?"

"Yes, sir, but I . . ."

"That's all right, son. I'll tell you. You ought to know. When you are grown you will have to work to make a living. All your life you'll have to work. Even if we were rich you would labor, because idleness is sinful. The Bible tells us that. I hope some day you will be able to work with your head, but first you've got to know how to work with your hands." The color of the ponderous clouds was deepening to blue and black. "No one is born knowing how to work. It is something we have to learn. You've got to learn to set your mind to a job and keep at it, no matter how hard it is or how long it takes or how much you dislike it. If you don't learn that you'll never amount to anything. And this is the time to learn it. Now do you know why you have to cut the grass?"

"Yes, sir."

"I don't like to make you work when you want to play, but it's for your own good. Can you understand that?"

"Yes, sir."

"Will you be a good boy and work hard this summer until the job is done?"

"Yes, sir."

I left the room feeling better. It was good to be forgiven, to be on good terms with one's father.

Day after day I worked in the yard, standing on my knees, cutting the grass close to the ground. There were few interruptions to break the monotony. Three or four times a day I went to the barn and sharpened the razor, but these trips were no escape. If I went too often or stayed too long my father took notice and put a stop to it. Many times each day I carried away the full basket of grass and stones, but the times of my departure and return were always observed. No evasions were possible because nothing escaped my father's eyes.

One day in July at noon I heard a rattle of dishes indicating that the table was being set. I was hot and tired and thirsty. I could smell the dinner cooking and thought of the tall glasses of iced tea. My mother came to the back door. At first I thought it was to call me, but it was only to throw out dishwater. Suddenly I dropped the razor and ran to the back steps.

"Mama," I called eagerly, but not loud enough for my father to hear. "Is dinner ready?"

"Yes, hon."

I came in, washed my hands, sat in the kitchen to wait.

"Son!"

It was my father's voice, the everlasting surveillance I could never escape.

"Yes, sir."

"What did you come in for?"

"Mama said dinner was ready."

"Did you *ask* her?"

"Yes, sir."

"You trifling scoundrel! Get on back outside to work! And wait till she *calls* you to dinner! You understand?"

As weeks passed the heat increased and the grass withered. Had a match been touched to it the work of a summer would have been accomplished in a few minutes. No rain fell, even for a day, to interrupt the work. The grass did not grow, and the ground which was cleared on the first day remained bare. The earth was baked to a depth of four or five feet and began to crack. The only living thing I encountered was an occasional spider climbing desperately in or out of the crevices in search of a habitable place. My friends knew I had to work and no longer came looking for me. Occasionally I would hear them playing in a nearby field, and sometimes in the mornings would see them pass with fishing poles over their shoulders. I knew that I was not missed, that they had stopped thinking of me and probably did not mention my name.

I became inured to the work but not reconciled to it, and throughout the summer continued to resist. Whippings—which had been rare before—were now common, and after each I would, in the evening, be required to apologize. I would go out on my father's glass porch, say I was sorry, and listen guiltily to a restatement of the principles involved. Tirelessly my father would explain what I had done wrong, the importance of learning to work, and the benefit to my character which this discipline would eventually bring about. After each of these sessions I would feel that I was innately lazy, unworthy, and impulsive. Each time I would resolve to try harder, to overcome my resentment, but each time would relapse. After two or three days I would again become sullen or rebellious and again would be punished. Sometimes I saw my mother in tears and knew she interceded in my behalf, but her efforts were ineffective.

Throughout June and July I worked every day except Sundays. As the job seemed endless I made no future plans. Anything that would last all summer was too large an obstacle to plan beyond; any happiness which lay at its end too remote to lift my spirit. About the middle of August, however, my outlook changed. One evening at sundown I noticed that relatively little grass remained standing. For the first time since the beginning of summer I realized that the job would have an end, that I would be free. Surveying the area remaining to be cut, I attempted to divide it by the area which could be cleared in a single day and reached an estimate of five days. I felt a surge of hope and began visualizing what I would do when I was through. During the next several days I worked faster and more willingly, but found that I had been too sanguine in my estimate. I did not finish on the fifth day or the sixth. But on the evening of the seventh it was apparent to my father as well as to me that the next day the job would be done. Only one or two hours of work remained.

The following morning—for the first time since May—
I woke to the sound of rain. I wanted to work anyway, to
get it over, but was told I could not. Then I asked if
I could go to Paul's house to play until the rain stopped.
Again the answer was no. About nine o'clock the rain let
up and I hurriedly began to work, but the lull was
brief and after a few minutes I had to stop. I stood under
the awning which extended out over the windows of my
father's porch and waited. After a while I sat on the ground
and leaned against the house. A half hour passed. The rain
was steady now, seemingly would last all day. It dripped
continuously from the canvas and formed a little trench in
the earth in front of my feet. I stared out at the gray sky
in a dull trance.

"I wish I could go to Paul's house."

I spoke in a low, sullen voice, hardly knowing whether
I was talking to myself or to my father.

"It's not fair not to let me play . . . just because it's rain-
ing. It's not fair at all."

There was no comment from above. Minutes passed.

"You're a mean bastard!"

A feeling of strangeness swept over me. I had never
cursed, was not used to such words. Something violent
was stirring in me, something long stifled was rankling
for expression.

"If you think you can kick me around all the time you're
wrong . . . you damned old bastard!"

At any moment I expected to be called. I would go
inside then and receive a whipping worse than I had
known possible. A minute passed in silence.

Could it be that my father had not heard? That seemed

unlikely, for always I spoke from this place and was always heard. The windows were open. There was nothing to prevent his hearing. Oh he had heard, all right. I was sure of that. Still, why wasn't I called? The waiting began to get on my nerves. Feeling that I could not make matters worse, I continued. This time I spoke louder and more viciously.

"You're the meanest man in the world. You lie up there in bed and are mean to everybody. I hate you!"

I began to feel astonished at myself. How incredible that I should be saying such things—I who had never dared a word of disrespect!

But why didn't he call? What was he waiting for? Was he waiting for me to say my worst so as to be able to whip me all the harder? The rain drizzled down. The day was gray and quiet. The whole thing began to seem unreal. The absence of reaction was as incredible as the defamation. Both seemed impossible. It was like a bad dream.

But it's real! I thought furiously. I *had* said those things, and would keep on saying them till I made him answer. I became frantic, poured out a tirade of abuse, searched my memory for every dirty word I knew, and when the store of profanity was exhausted and I stopped, breathless, to listen . . . there was no response.

"You goddamn dirty son of a bitch!" I screamed, "I wish you was dead! I wish you was dead, do you hear? Do you hear me?"

I had finished. Now something would happen. I cowered and waited for it, but there was no word from the porch. Not a sound. Not even the stir of bedclothes.

The rage passed and I became miserable. I sat with

arms around my knees, staring blankly at the indifferent rain. As the minutes went by I became more appalled by what I had done. Its meaning broadened, expanded in endless ramifications, became boundless and unforgivable. I had broken the commandment to honor thy father and mother. I had taken the name of the Lord in vain, and that was the same as cursing God. I thought of my mother. What would she say when she learned? I pictured her face. She would cry.

For another half hour I sat there. I no longer expected to be called. For some reason the matter was to be left in abeyance. Finally, unable to endure further waiting, I got up and walked away. I went to the barn and wandered about morosely, expecting momentarily to see my mother enter to say that my father wanted me, but she did not come, and the morning passed without further incident.

On entering the house for dinner my first concern was to learn whether she knew. When she smiled I knew that she did not. Now that I was indoors I knew something would happen. I stayed as far from the porch as possible and spoke in low tones. Yet my father must know me to be present. I could not eat, and soon left the house and went back to the barn, where I felt somewhat less vulnerable.

I spent the afternoon there alone, sitting on a box, waiting. Occasionally I would get up and walk around aimlessly. Sometimes I would stand in the doorway looking out at the rain. Though unrestrained I felt myself a prisoner. I searched through my small understanding of my father but found no explanation of the delay. It was unlike him to postpone a whipping. Then it occurred to me that what I had done might so far exceed ordinary transgression as to require a special punishment. Perhaps I would not be whipped at all but sent away from home, never be permitted to come back.

When supper time came I sneaked into the house and tried to be inconspicuous, but was so agitated that my mother was concerned. She looked at me inquiringly and ran her hand affectionately through my hair. "What's the matter, son? Don't you feel well? You look haggard."

"I feel all right," I said.

I escaped her and sat alone on the back porch until called to the table. When supper was safely over my situation was unimproved. It was too late to go outside again, and I could not long remain in the house without meeting my father. At the latest it could be put off only till family prayer. Perhaps that was the time when my crime would be related. Maybe they would pray for me and then expel me from home. I had just begun drying the dishes when the long-awaited sound was heard.

"Son."

It was not the wrathful voice I had expected. It was calm, just loud enough to be audible. Nevertheless it was enough to make me tremble and drop a spoon. For a moment it seemed I could not move.

"Your daddy wants you, dear."

I put down the dishtowel and went to the door of the porch.

"Yes, sir."

"Come out here where I can see you."

I approached the bed. My hands were clenched and I was biting my lip, trying not to cry.

"Your mother tells me you haven't been eating well today. You aren't sick, are you?"

"No, sir."

"You feel all right?"

"Yes, sir."

"Sit down, son. I just called you out here to talk for a while. I often think we don't talk to each other enough. I guess that's my fault. We'll have to do better in the future. I'd like to hear more about what you're interested in and what you think, because that's the only way I can get to know you." He paused a moment. "Maybe you think because I'm grown up I understand everything, but that's not true. You'll find as you get older that no matter how much you learn there's always much you don't know. For example you're my own son and I ought to know you pretty well, but every now and then something'll happen that'll make me realize I don't understand you at all."

I choked back a sob and tried to brace myself for the coming blow.

"I don't think I ever understood my own father," he went on presently, "until it was too late. We were very poor—much poorer, son, than you can imagine. From year in to year out we might see only a few dollars in our house, and what little there was had to be saved for essentials. When we sold our cotton we'd have to buy a plow or an ax. And there were staple foods we had to buy like flour and sugar. We bought cloth, too, but never any ready-made clothes. Until I was a grown man I never had any clothes except what my mother made. I got my first store-bought suit to go away to medical school in, and I don't believe my mother ever had a store-bought dress. My father worked hard and made his boys work hard. We resented it and sometimes even hated him for it, but in the end we knew he was right. One of my brothers never could get along with Daddy, and he ran away from home when he was fifteen. He turned out to be a no-account scoundrel, and the last I heard of him he was a saloon keeper in New Orleans.

"In the summer we hoed corn and picked cotton, and in the winter we fixed rail fences and chopped wood and hauled it home. And always there were mules and pigs to take care of. It was a very different life from yours . . . and in some ways a better one." He looked at me affectionately. "At any rate, we learned how to work, and there's nothing more important for a boy to learn. It's something you haven't yet learned, son. Isn't that right?"

"Yes, sir."

"You will, though. If you ever amount to anything you'll learn. You're learning now. I wish you could understand, though, that I wouldn't be trying to teach you so fast if I knew I would live long enough to teach you more slowly." He paused a moment. "Do you have anything to say?"

"No, sir."

"Then I guess you'd better see if your mother needs you."

I stood up, hardly able to believe that this was all.

"Son."

"Yes, sir."

"Come here a minute."

I went to the bed and my father put a hand on my shoulder. "Remember, son," he said in a husky voice, "whenever it seems I'm being hard on you . . . it's because I love you."

Late that night I woke in terror from a nightmare. For several minutes I lay in bed trembling, unable to convince myself that it was just a dream. Presently I got up and tiptoed through the dark house to the porch.

"Daddy?" I whispered. "Daddy . . . are you all right?"

There was no reply, but soon I became aware of his regular breathing. I went back to bed but almost immediately got up and knelt on the floor. "Dear God, please don't let anything happen to Daddy. Amen."

Still I could not sleep. I lay in bed and thought of many things and after a while began worrying about the razor. What had I done with it? Was it still on the ground under the awning? Perhaps I had left it open. Someone might step on it and get cut. I got up again and went outside looking for it. In the dark I felt about on the ground under my father's windows but did not find it. Then I went to the barn and found it in its usual place, properly closed.

The next morning before noon I finished the job. The last blade of grass was cut and carried away and the back yard was as bald as a razor could make it.

"Daddy," I said, standing under the porch windows, "I've finished. Is it all right?"

He looked over the yard, then took his binoculars and scrutinized it in more detail, particularly the corners.

"That's well done, son."

I put away the basket and razor and came inside. After dinner I began to feel uncomfortable. It seemed strange not to be working. Restless, unable to sit still, I wandered about the house, looking out the windows and wondering what to do. Presently I sought and obtained permission to go to Paul's house, but somehow felt I was doing something wrong.

During the next two weeks I often played with my friends but never fully lost myself in play and was secretly glad when school started and life settled down to a routine again. I was more quiet than before and better behaved, and when next the report cards were distributed I had a nearly perfect score in conduct.

VI

THE VISION
OF CHANGE

My father and I have never parted. He made his mark on me that summer, and after his death that fall continued to speak on a high-fidelity system within my conscience, speaks to me still, tells me that I have been summoned, that I am standing once again before him on that glass porch giving an account of myself, that I will be found wanting, still after all these years a "low-down, no-account scoundrel," and that this judgment will be binding on my view, that I shall not now or ever be permitted to regard myself as innocent or worthy.

These things, accepted as true, make one a slave, have so made me and make me still, fifty years after those pale blue eyes have gone to the grave. Whenever a current situation calls upon me to stand forth, to present myself, my father speaks again with undiminished authority. His denunciation yields guilt and anxiety, tends to drive me out of human society into the wilderness alone, thereby to confirm ever more deeply the image of myself as unworthy to live with others, having nothing to say, deserving of no recognition. To accept that image altogether is to die; I have accepted it in part, have found in the writing of books a fearful way of denying it. From exile I send back messages: "I'm still here!" "Don't forget me!" "I *do* have something to say. Please recognize me!"

What seemed like freedom begins to look like illness. I see myself as a cripple, forced off the main path of human affairs. Friends come to dinner: Martin is just back from a symposium in Madrid organized by a drug company, regales us with tales of festivities. No one heard his paper, he says, too much eating and drinking. I note my interest in that observation, as if I were *glad* he had not been heard, suspect myself of envy. Howard has been invited to give the Woodrow Wilson Lectures at Princeton. Only three months away, and he's not prepared, has nothing to say of an originality up to the occasion. I am smug at his unease, as if I might *want* him to fail, again sense envy. It has been there all along, I now think, unnoticed behind my glib declaration that I do not myself *want* such things. That not wanting, I now know, is deeply unreliable, for whereas it presents itself as preference it is rather the deflection of preference by fear. More than deflection, perhaps a turnabout; for I have allowed this anxiety to become an absolute barrier, in imagination have been declining invitations to speak on occasions which are all but forcing, as at the funeral of a friend.

Funeral of a friend! Now there's a giveaway. No doubt I want all my prominent friends to die! What I must deny myself, they shall not live to enjoy. I will stand mute at their funerals, and when they are all gone, only then will spite be sated and envy stilled. What a bag of worms is man!

My father's way with me accounts for more. Not only *that* I write, but what I write. And not only what I write, but the conclusions I come to. I begin to see answers to questions I had not even thought to ask. Why am I always writing about freedom? Why this crusade to destroy the credibility of determinism? Is this the free choice of an unfettered mind selecting a subject for its inherent interest only? Or have I been led to it by an invisible hand, to the conclusions I have arrived at by an inaudible voice?

A man in chains need not be a slave. If he has pride and self-respect he is a free man though a prisoner, and a constant danger to his jailers. Conversely, a slave who escapes is not a free man, but a runaway slave who may be caught and returned to servitude. A slave is one who accepts the identity ascribed to him by a master: "You are an inferior and unworthy person and so will remain, and therefore must serve me with obedience and humility." As we can record on tape the radio signal of a voice—record directly from receiver to tape without intermediate translation into sound waves—so now I continue silently, inaudibly, to receive and record that message from my father who, having even in heaven nothing better to do, continues to send: "You are a lazy, low-down, no-account scoundrel!"

I do not credit him with the craft I now perceive in his ways with me. He cannot have figured it out, had rather an infallible instinct, was a genius. The danger to a master is that a slave will revolt and in that revolt create and secure the identity of a free man. Yet on the one occasion when my resentment burst forth in an assertion of my worth and in denunciation of the master, my father found a way of handling it so demoniacally accurate that even this rebellion was shown to me to be further and ever more conclusive evidence of my inferiority and unworthiness.

Thus I was made a psychological slave. In the presence of people I become sweaty, want to run away, as if not deserving the company of normal people.

The last notes of Brahms' Second Symphony. An intermission of fifteen minutes. In the crowded aisle I see Mrs. Crowthers and Mrs. Walsh. At one time they were my patients, and I retain a special meaning for them. They greet me shyly, I greet them warmly. Both are artists, charming and talented women. I am fond of them. Slowly we proceed up the crowded aisle together. I ask about their children, their work. They are immensely pleased to be chatting with me. We reach the lobby. Now there is more room, we will be able to stand at ease, to converse. I am alone, cannot conceal my driven isolation behind my wife's sociability. "I have to go upstairs," I say to them. "Please excuse me. It has been awfully good to see you." I shake hands, bow, depart. They are disappointed.

So what then? I find a deserted corner, sit alone. One might think I had escaped from bores, but I would have loved to talk with them. I find no pleasure in this isolation, only a weird safety, an obscure shame. If a slave should find himself in the drawing room with the master he would feel as I felt a few moments ago; and when, abashed at being so out of place, he should escape to the slave quarters he would feel as I feel now. I remember sitting out that terrible rainy day in the barn.

I am a runaway slave who has become an escape artist, have all these years liked to think that I live and work alone in freedom in my silent room, that I live as I live, and do as I do, by free choice. But this freely chosen solitude I now see as hiding, and always I am in danger of being caught, as by those ladies at the concert, whereupon panic tells me I retain the identity inscribed by my father.

So is it really so spontaneous, my forever writing about the metaphysics of freedom? Can it be taken at face value, the subtlety with which I undermine determinism? Is it not rather shadow play for a more ancient drama, a sublimated rebellion against my unacknowledged servitude? Might I not do better, even as an old man, to go back to that sea of grass, to sit once more under that awning, in that ancient drizzle of unforgotten rain, and once more scream invective at the tyrant overhead? Our Father who art in Heaven, damned be thy name!

General Patton recalls an incident which occurred during the Argonne offensive of 1918 in the midst of heavy fighting: "I felt a great desire to run, I was trembling with fear when suddenly I thought of my progenitors and seemed to see them in a cloud over the German lines looking at me. I became calm at once and saying aloud 'It is time for another Patton to die' . . . went forward to what I honestly believed to be certain death."[1]

The touching stuffiness of that word "progenitors," the touching appeal of that "honestly." I envy him his "pro-

1. Martin Blumenson, *The Patton Papers 1885–1940* (Boston: Houghton, Mifflin Company, 1972).

genitors" who come down from heaven to help him go forward; mine accuse me of cowardice, predict I will run.

Always I turn away from anger as petty and mean, destructive of life, and so it is often, but not always. There is another kind of anger, different in quality, in implication, in consequence; when one beholds it one sees nothing ugly but something grand. Sviatoslav Richter strides out on the stage. His face is grim; there is anger in the set of his jaw, but not at the audience. This is a passion altogether his own, a force with which he protects what he is about to do. If it had words it would say, "What I attempt is important and I go about it with utmost seriousness. I intend to create beauty and meaning, and everything everywhere threatens this endeavor: the coughs, the latecomers, the chatting woman in the third row, and always those dangers within, distraction, confusion, loss of memory, weakness of hand. All are enemies of my endeavor. I call up this passion to oppose them, to protect my purpose." Now he begins to play, and the anger I see in his bearing I hear in the voice of Beethoven. It knows nothing of meanness or spite; it is the passion of the doer who will not let his work be swept aside. It hurts no one, it asserts life, it is the force that generates form. Its opposite is not love but weakness.

When next I feel those steel fingers close around my heart I must seek a division of self, must find a way of turning around inside, as it were, to discover those pale blue eyes still fixed upon me, and to reject at last the ancient accusation, must face my father who now is the condemning part of self, and say, "It is *you* who is the enemy, not those out there. It is *you* who would destroy me!"

In danger I will feel either fear or anger, and either may be self-preserving. If I am to avoid danger by running, fear will help me run faster; if I am to stand my ground, anger will help me stand it more firmly. In this neurotic danger, since I intend not to run, fear is useless, worse than useless, is itself the greatest hazard. Anger is what I need. To cringe before that inner denunciation is to perpetuate the past, to reaffirm my father's authority to determine how I regard myself. All these years his judgment has held sway; now I must find a way, without tearing the whole house down, to rise up against him, to seek him out who now is part of me, who still wordlessly condemns me as unworthy. If I have something to say and mean it I must stand behind it, must mobilize a dark and deep-running anger to protect it.

VII

THE UPWARD SPIRAL

How curious, though, that this perception of the determining quality of childhood experience is at the same time the creation of freedom. The insights by which I now see real slavery behind illusory freedom do not themselves fall within the field of events perceived as determined, but constitute a new vantage point, something apart from the experience being examined, a psychological space platform where before was but a void. From it emanate strategies, influences.

My condition of slavery, by virtue of my recognition of its cause, is enabled to escape that causality. I see ways of doing battle, of overcoming that subjugation, and, though no victory is to be claimed in advance, the exposure of causality makes it vulnerable to change. For what has made my father's voice so irresistible all these years, his judgment of me so implacably my destiny, has been the continuing silent and unnoticed reception of his message. So soon as I translate it into audible sound it becomes feasible for me to disagree, to become if need be vehement and angry in disagreement. I have resources beyond those of that child under the awning, and if the old drama now takes place visibly and audibly these resources become for the first time available to me, may achieve a different outcome. Those insights which so convincingly portray my life as determined enable me to intervene in that causality, to bring it about that those forces which necessarily made me what I am, and held me so long in that being, no longer achieve this end. The demonstration of necessity is simultaneously the proof of freedom.

So it is possible to change something that was determined in such a way as to be unchangeable. Where may we find the logic in this paradox?

Suppose I now consider the foregoing inquiry into the sources of anxiety as I then considered the anxiety itself, namely as a "thing" to be examined. Is it not possible that I might arrive at comparable findings? Namely, that whereas I had had a feeling of freedom in the investigation, of being receptive to anything that might turn up, in fact I had been conditioned in such a way that only certain things *could* turn up, or *would* strike me as relevant, that therefore I was *bound* both to make the inquiry and to arrive at the results I did arrive at? And that someone else, differently conditioned, a Jungian analyst, for example, would have arrived at different findings?

I have taken a segment of experience, A (my present way of life, its isolation, its anxieties), as an object for investigation. The investigation itself has now become another segment of my experience, B (a body of insight into the causal relations between my present way of life and remote encounters with my father). The first segment, A, appeared free at the beginning of the second segment, B. Now, the second segment having come into being, the first segment is seen as determined, the necessary outcome of childhood conditioning. Yet the proof by B that the apparent freedom of A was illusory, that A was in fact determined, has now the effect of creating a *real* freedom in A: the understanding of how something was necessarily brought about becomes the means to change it.

We may inquire now, in like manner, into the freedom or necessity of B. B is that segment of experience which came into being as a consequence of my taking A as an object of inquiry. B, it appears, was free from the beginning and remains free. That is to say, nothing *required* that the inquiry be undertaken, and, having been undertaken, nothing required that these particular findings be arrived at. This assertion of the freedom of B is but the ordinary assumption of scientific objectivity: the scientist considers himself free to arrive at any conclusion his observations suggest, assumes that he is not pre-set on a course which makes him bound to arrive at a certain understanding of the phenomena in question regardless of what his observations indicate. Indeed the whole idea of scientific investigation is to avoid that kind of predetermined thinking, to bring it about that we are truly free to see what is really there. In asserting such freedom for B, however, I must recall that A, too, seemed free at the start, just as self-evidently free as B now seems. If I could be so mistaken about A, could I not be similarly mistaken about B?

The spirit of science is not to prejudge, but to give any honest query a fair shake. A fair shake in this instance is to take *B* as an object of investigation, which then would create another segment of experience, *C*, from which indeed it might eventually transpire that *B* was just as fully determined as had been *A*. It might be demonstrated, for example, that all those insights which comprise *B* were contingent upon the investigator having been a psychoanalyst, or indeed upon his having been a twentieth-century man, and that the same inquiry into the same phenomena of the same life, conducted by a mystic or by a medieval scholar, would have arrived at findings of quite a different order. The apparent freedom of *B* would then stand revealed as having actually been determined, and the same paradox would then be reenacted at one level higher up: the demonstration by *C* that *B* was really determined would make it possible for *B* then to become really free; for the insights of *C* would suggest ways in which the constraints which had operated unnoticed on *B* could be circumvented. *C* would have become one further psychological space platform from which would emanate the freedom to change the realm of *B*. And *C* itself could, of course, become the object of some further investigation.

Something lies behind us, something goes before us; consciousness lies between. We look back and see what we are as having been determined, thereby creating the freedom whereby to elude that determination. The necessity which shaped us in the past came in time to operate within us as a rule of mental operation—not something that mind *knows* or creates, but something that mind *is*, something it-self beyond the reach of mind. I receive an invitation to lecture, I automatically decline—this is the rule of mental operation. I think it is something I choose to *do* but it is something rather I have come to *be*. Though accompanied by a feeling of freedom it is deeply determined. Now this rule of mental operation which once was metaconscious becomes conscious, and the exposing of that necessity, of that ancient authority that authored the rule, creates the freedom whereby that necessity may be eluded. At the same time we must suppose that the insight which creates this freedom might be treated likewise and might there-upon be shown to follow comparable rules, now meta-conscious, created by comparable conditioning.

An idea, like the contact of tossed pebble with surface of pond, is a wave which moves outward, expanding, in-teracting with wave fronts of other ideas, gradually making contact with the entire intellectual universe. At the moment of its birth, the idea is an explosion subject to no rule. Even-tually it may be studied retrospectively, along with other related ideas, and made subject perhaps to some law of in-tellectual development. But the law which then explains the occurrence of those ideas will not explain the law which is itself a different wave, further on. Our psychological universe expands as does the physical universe. Both are open systems.

Being the product of conditioning and being free to change do not war with each other. Both are true. They coexist, grow together in an upward spiral, and the growth of one furthers the growth of the other. The more cogently we prove ourselves to have been shaped by causes, the more opportunities we create for changing. The more we change, the more possible it becomes to see how determined we were in that which we have just ceased to be.

What makes a battleground of these two points of view is to conceive of either as an absolute which excludes the other. For when the truth of either view is extended to the point of excluding the truth of the other it becomes not only false but incoherent. We must affirm freedom and responsibility without denying that we are the product of circumstance, and must affirm that we are the product of circumstance without denying that we have the freedom to transcend that causality to become something which could not even have been previsioned from the circumstances which shaped us. What destroys the behaviorist's argument is not the evidence marshaled to demonstrate that we are controlled by environment—that is utterly convincing—but the use of that evidence to deny freedom.

We may not ask how, in accounting for ourselves, we are to apportion the influence of freedom and the influence of shaping circumstance. We cannot combine them as measured vectors to arrive at the trajectory of our lives. During experience in process each view finds its limit in the other, yet neither view ultimately is limited by anything short of the complete range of experience. No reasonable division can be made, not because the proportion assigned to each would be arbitrary but because either view may legitimately claim the whole field.

The relation is one of complete alternativity: we are altogether free to do as we choose, and we are altogether determined to do as we do. In greatest constraint—as in mounting a scaffold to be hanged—it is always possible to do other than one does: if walking, we might refuse to walk and be dragged; if silent, we might be singing or screaming; if weeping we might be laughing. Likewise, in enjoyment of greatest freedom it is always possible to create a vantage point from which that freedom may be seen as caused. The realm of experience is not, therefore, to be divided like Ireland into the free and the ruled. The distinction is hierarchic. Any realm can, in principle, be demonstrated as determined, and in this process there will be created another realm, hierarchically removed, which is free and which then may free the first realm which has just been proven to have been determined.

In a condition of struggle and of failure we must be able to say "I must try harder" or "I must try differently." Both views are essential; neither must take precedence by principle. They are analogous to the view of man as free and the view of man as determined. The two do not contend, but reflect the interaction between man and his environment. A change in either makes for a change in outcome. When we say "I must try harder" we mean that the most relevant variable is something within us—intention, will, determination, "meaning it"—and that if this changes, the outcome, even if everything else remain unchanged, will be different. When we say "I must try differently" we mean that the most relevant variable lies in the situation within which intention is being exerted, that we should look to the environment, to the ways it pushes and pulls at us, and in this study find the means to alter that interaction.

We try to stop smoking, try and fail, try again and fail again, and when we pause to reflect, to ask how we should understand the recurrent failure, we must regard it from both views. If we believe we cannot try harder, then we must examine the field in which the effort is being made, look for ways to diminish the obstacles against which will is pitted. If we conclude there is nothing to be altered in the field, we must go back to the possibility of augmenting intention. We cannot know the outcome in advance. If we give up, we can never know but that further trying—either harder or differently—might have succeeded. If we succeed, the last move is likely to take all the credit. "I tried will power for years," one man will say, "and I can tell you it doesn't work. But when I left my desk in that travel agency and took a job on a ranch—right away I stopped. No sweat." "I tried all kinds of tricks," another man will say, "smoking substitutes, pills, poisoned cigarettes, not going to cocktail parties . . . all delaying tactics. Finally I got sick of it and asked myself straight out, 'Listen, you jerk! Do you mean it or not?' Then I meant it, and then I stopped."

There is a fundamental difference between such questions as "What is the nature of electricity?" and "What is the nature of man?" In the former a high degree of objectivity, though never absolute, may be maintained; a scientist who likes electricity may concur with one who is afraid of it. No such objectivity is possible concerning the nature of man; for the inquirer is part of the object of inquiry, and his purposes affect what is found. If, therefore, we are to have rational discourse about man we must know the context in which our questions arise, whether they refer to individuals or to societies, and the purposes and assumptions of the questioner.

A black youth, gun in hand, cowers in the darkened doorway of a locked store. The police officer, gun in holster, comes toward him. "Stay away from me, pig!" "Drop that gun, punk." "Stop! Pig!" "Drop that. . . ." The shot kills the officer, and four months later the black youth stands in court. He has no gun now, is wearing a jacket and tie, is being judged. Judge on the bench, jury in the box, bailiffs, clerks, security officers, the public in attendance— all the procedures of hearing evidence, of establishing facts, of recording testimony, of taking an appeal. Testimony is heard. Witnesses establish that the defendant fired the fatal shot. Psychiatrists state that he is and was sane, that is, knew the nature and consequences of his act.

Before a verdict is rendered, the defendant speaks in his own defense. Let us ascribe to him unlimited verbal and logical ability in order that we may imagine all possible modes of defense.

"The cause of crime," he might say, "is poverty. 'Inescapably, the poor commit crimes,' writes Richard Harris, 'sometimes out of resentment, sometimes out of laziness, or sometimes out of need, but most of all because they live in a society where they find little besides poverty, sickness, and violence and are rarely exposed to any traditional moral standards. Today, most of those who commit the crimes that are most feared—assault, rape, murder—are black. . . . If a third of all young black men cannot get work and cannot earn enough money, say, to buy a suit of clothes or even enough to take a girl out for a movie and a glass of beer, they are likely to steal. And if they have little hope of ever getting a decent job, they will likely turn to drugs to ease their frustration and bitterness. Then, of course, they will have to steal more. Since very little is being done to provide training or work for them the results seem inevitable."[1] I, Your Honor, am a victim of this neglect. I have been unable to obtain work. I have lived for years in an overcrowded and rat-infested tenement. I am unmarried because I have never had enough money to take a girl to the movies or out for a beer, and I see little prospect of my ever being able to support a family. These circumstances so embittered me that my action was inevitable."

The judge, if we ascribe to him not only a sense of fairness but an equal ability in logic, might reply as follows: "There is merit in what you say, and I am in sympathy with the tenor of your remarks. I must point out, however, that you are calling upon this court to make a judgment upon society and, in consequence of that judgment, to find you innocent. Although the judgment on society which you propose may be just, this court is not empowered to make it. Your remarks, therefore, in this context are irrelevant."

1. Richard Harris, "The New Justice," *The New Yorker*, March 25, 1972, p. 45.

The defendant is silent, then with a devious expression speaks as follows: "Many eminent thinkers take a rather different view of the problem of crime," he says. "The solution, they say—again I quote Richard Harris—'lies in enacting stricter new laws, applying unused old laws, imposing longer sentences, and making prisons so disagreeable, despite all the current talk about prison reform, that their occupants won't want to be sent back to them once they get out. For some years, Richard Nixon has been the leading proponent of this view. In the 1968 presidential campaign, he repeatedly called for a crackdown on lawbreakers, and offered his solution: "If the conviction rate were doubled in this country, it would do more to eliminate crime in the future than a quadrupling of the funds for any governmental war on poverty.' "[2] As Your Honor, more than anyone else, is aware, such recommendations have not been followed. Capital punishment has virtually disappeared, and a reasonably intelligent young black man such as I, particularly one gifted with my verbal ability, can be certain of a light sentence, can know that soon he will be out on parole. Realizing this, I lacked sufficient countermotivation to oppose my motive to steal and to kill. Society is at fault, having failed to generate effective inhibitions."

"I am somewhat less in sympathy with this view," the judge replies. "Its merit, however, or lack of merit, need not detain us; for, like the former view, it is an indictment of society. I must remind you again, with diminishing patience, that this court is not empowered to judge society

2. *Ibid.*, p. 44.

and that any judgment you might make upon it, however accurate and, in other circumstances, appropriate, is in this context irrelevant."

The defendant becomes more serious as his jeopardy deepens. "Virtually every philosopher of the Modern Age," he says, "has concluded that free will is but the name we give to a subjective sense of choice which has no objective reality, that the measure of freedom we ascribe to man measures only our ignorance of the forces that move us. 'An intelligence,' writes Laplace, 'knowing, at a given instant of time, all forces acting in nature, as well as the momentary positions of all things of which the universe consists, would be able to comprehend the motions of the largest bodies of the world and those of the smallest atoms in one single formula, provided it were sufficiently powerful to subject the data to analysis. To it, nothing would be uncertain, both future and past would be present before its eyes.' I am what I am, Your Honor, by virtue of all those forces which shaped me, and every transient thought and every slightest act, even that twitch of trigger finger, is the inexorable outcome of preexisting forces and so, however alterable it may *appear* to have been, was in fact predetermined and inalterable. I am innocent because, according to the deepest convictions of our scientific age, I could not have acted otherwise."

"This defense," the judge replies, "unlike your two previous efforts, *is* relevant. Were the court to accept your argument it would find you innocent. Or, more accurately, would rule against itself, concluding that verdicts of guilty or innocent have themselves lost meaning.

"Your defense is disallowed, however, because the court does not accept this view of man. The mechanistic model as extended to the entire universe, including ourselves, has never been accepted by anybody in his actual daily life, not even by the mechanistic philosophers of whom you speak, and no court of law certainly has ever accepted that view. We hold that you were free to pull the trigger as you did, or to drop the gun as you did not, that such freedom is at the very heart of what we believe man to be, and that no conceivable examination of forces acting upon you at that moment or at any other moment in your life, even if in fineness and precision this examination could be extended to include the coordinates and excursions of every atom in your brain, or indeed of the entire universe, could reveal evidence proving that you were compelled to do one rather than the other. We hold therefore that you were a free agent, that you could have done either, that you are the author of what you did do and so must be responsible for your act. We find you guilty."

After a term in prison, let us assume, the black youth is determined to change—an unlikely attitude in view of the degree to which prisons are not "correctional facilities," as they are called, but factories of crime, and assumed here only to examine the logic of attitudes toward change—and to this end has undertaken psychotherapy. He calls upon the judge, says, "In order that I shall never again commit a crime I am undertaking to find out why I *did* commit that one. I'm going to examine, and hope eventually to understand, not only why I pulled that trigger, but also why I was breaking into that store, in a larger sense why I became a person who steals. For although my circumstances were deprived, not everybody from such circumstances turns to crime. Why did I? What were the forces that pushed me? These things I must learn to the end that it not happen again." The judge, without the slightest inconsistency, may endorse this view and applaud this decision.

We cannot hope to find a view of man that will be independent of the context in which we find ourselves, the purposes we follow, the assumptions we make. Sometimes it will be necessary to see behavior, individual or social, as the product of preexisting conditions, for we are indeed pushed and pulled, and if we are to increase our authority in reference to these forces we must examine them as causes. Sometimes, likewise, it will be necessary to see behavior, individual or social, as the product of unconstrained will, for we are truly free, even in situations of extreme coercion.

It should not be, therefore, that some of us such as judges and parole officers always see behavior as a product of free will, while others such as social scientists and behavioral psychologists always see it as controlled by environment, but that each of us is capable of both views, realizing that in some contexts one view is indicated, in other contexts the other, that we need never, therefore, and must not ever, assert the truth of one view to the exclusion of the truth of the other.

VIII

THE LIMITS
OF CHANGE

Sometimes in therapy profound change occurs spontaneously, without effort or intention. It is a rare experience—any time, anywhere—to be known and understood without being judged, to be regarded with affection and respect, without being used. No therapist can feel this way about all his patients, though he must try. When he does genuinely so feel, he creates a nurturing context in which the patient may take in and make his own the therapist's way of thinking about problems, a certain reflectiveness about suffering, a tendency to hold conflicting motives in suspension while looking for connections, meanings, significance.

Such identification leads to slight, subtle, often unnoticed changes in action and behavior, in one's ways of dealing with one's self and others; and over a period of time these changed actions may achieve a change of being. One then feels one's self to be profoundly different without knowing how or why. If one is asked, "Well, what did you learn? What was the main insight?" one may stumble about, fabricate some inadequate answer, yet may know certainly that one is a better person, more able to love.

This sort of change is rare. We can't count on it, can't make it happen; when it occurs it is great good fortune, a bonus. Usually change—when it occurs at all—follows long and arduous trying.

Neurotic suffering indicates inner conflict. Each side of the conflict is likely to be a composite of many partial forces, each one of which has been structured into behavior, attitude, perception, value. Each component asserts itself, claims priority, insists that something else yield, accommodate. The conflict therefore is fixed, stubborn, enduring. It may be impugned and dismissed without effect, imprecations and remorse are of no avail, strenuous acts of will may be futile; it causes—yet survives and continues to cause—the most intense suffering, humiliation, rending of flesh. Such a conflict is not to be uprooted or excised. It is not an ailment, it is the patient himself. The suffering will not disappear without a change in the conflict, and a change in the conflict amounts to a change in what one is and how one lives, feels, reacts.

Personality is a complex balance of many conflicting claims, forces, tensions, compunctions, distractions, which yet manages somehow to be a functioning entity. However it may have come to be what it is, it resists becoming anything else. It tends to maintain itself, to convey itself onward into the future unaltered. It may be changed only with difficulty. It may be changed from within, spontaneously and unthinkingly, by an onslaught of physiological force, as in adolescence. It may be changed from without, again spontaneously and unthinkingly, by the force of unusual circumstance, as in a Nazi concentration camp. And sometimes it may be changed from within, deliberately, consciously, and by design. Never easily, never for sure, but slowly, uncertainly, and only with effort, insight, and a kind of tenacious creative cunning.

Personality change follows change in behavior. Since we are what we do, if we want to change what we are we must begin by changing what we do, must undertake a new mode of action. Since the import of such action is change it will run afoul of existing entrenched forces which will protest and resist. The new mode will be experienced as difficult, unpleasant, forced, unnatural, anxiety-provoking. It may be undertaken lightly but can be sustained only by considerable effort of will. Change will occur only if such action is maintained over a long period of time.

The place of insight is to illumine: to ascertain where one is, how one got there, how now to proceed, and to what end. It is a blueprint, as in building a house, and may be essential, but no one achieves a house by blueprints alone, no matter how accurate or detailed. A time comes when one must take up hammer and nails. In building a house the making of blueprints may be delegated to an architect, the construction to a carpenter. In building the house of one's life or in its remodeling, one may delegate nothing; for the task can be done, if at all, only in the workshop of one's own mind and heart, in the most intimate rooms of thinking and feeling where none but one's self has freedom of movement or competence or authority. The responsibility lies with him who suffers, originates with him, remains with him to the end. It will be no less his if he enlists the aid of a therapist; we are no more the product of our therapists than of our genes: we create ourselves. The sequence is suffering, insight, will, action, change. The one who suffers, who wants to change, must bear responsibility all the way. "Must" because so soon as responsibility is ascribed, the forces resisting change occupy the whole of one's being, and the process of change comes to a halt. A psychiatrist may help, perhaps crucially, but his best help will be of no avail if he is required to provide a kind or degree of insight which will of itself achieve change.

Should an honest man wish to become a thief the necessary action is obvious: he must steal—not just once or occasionally, but frequently, consistently, taking pains that the business of planning and executing thefts replace other activities which in implication might oppose the predatory life. If he keeps at it long enough his being will conform to his behavior; he will have become a thief. Conversely, should a thief undertake to become an honest man, he must stop stealing and must undertake actions which replace stealing, not only in time and energy, and perhaps also excitement, but which carry implications contrary to the predatory life, that is, productive or contributive activities. If a homosexual man should set out to become heterosexual, among all that is obscure, two things are clear: he should discontinue homosexual relations, however much tempted he may be to continue on an occasional spontaneous basis, and he should undertake, continue, and maintain heterosexual relations, however

little heart he may have for women, however often he fail,
and however inadequate and averse he may find himself
to be. He would be well advised in reaching for such a
goal to anticipate that success, if it be achieved at all, will
require a long time, years not months, that the effort will
be painful and humiliating, that he will discover profound
currents of feeling which oppose the behavior he now
requires of himself, that emerging obstacles will each one
seem insuperable yet each must be thought through, that
further insight will be constantly required to inform and
sustain his behavior, that sometimes insight will precede
and illumine action, and sometimes blind dogged action
must come first, and that even so, with the best of will
and good faith and determination, he still may fail. He
should beware of beckoning shortcuts, such as drug therapy or hypnosis. They falsify the reality with which he
must most intimately deal, that of his own thought, feeling,
drive; they undermine his commitment of internal resources by encouraging him to feel that there is an easier
way. There is no short cut, no safe-conduct, no easier way.
He must proceed alone, on nerve. He is not entitled to
much hope—just that he has a chance. He may take some
bleak comfort only in knowing that no one can be sure
at the outset that he will fail, and that it is his own un-
measured and unmeasurable resources of heart and mind
and will which have most bearing on the eventual outcome.

This is self-transcendence and is not to be confused
with a type of coercive treatment in which the therapist

acts as agent for society, and the goal is adjustment. Punishment, brainwashing, and lobotomy fall in this category. Less extreme varieties are known variously as operant conditioning, behavior therapy, or conditioned reflex therapy. All such treatment takes the person as object and seeks to achieve the desired change by manipulation. The alcoholic may be so rigged with wires as to receive an electric shock each time he takes a drink. The homosexual man may be provided with male partners who insure that sexual experiences will be exceedingly unpleasant, and, concurrently, with gently seductive women, without demands of their own, who introduce him to the delights of polarized sexuality. Such things may be arranged for a fee.

We are in no position to comment on the efficacy of behavior therapy as generally practiced, but in principle we know it works. People may indeed be treated as objects and may be profoundly affected thereby. Kick a dog often enough and he will become cowardly or vicious. People who are kicked undergo similar changes; their view of the world and of themselves is transformed. The survivors of Hitler's concentration camps testify that the treatment received did have an effect. Nor find we reason to doubt the alleged results of Chinese thought-control methods. People may indeed be brainwashed, for benign or exploitative reasons.

Behavior therapy is not, therefore, being contrasted with self-transcendence in terms of efficacy; the contrast is in terms of freedom. If one's destiny is shaped by manipulation one has become more of an object, less of a subject, has lost freedom. It matters little whether the manipulation is known to the person upon whom it acts. For even if one himself designs and provides for those experiences which are then to affect him, he is nevertheless treating himself as object—and to some extent, therefore, *becomes* an object.

If, however, one's destiny is shaped from within then one has become more of a creator, has gained freedom. This is self-transcendence, a process of change that originates in one's heart and expands outward, always within the purview and direction of a knowing consciousness, begins with a vision of freedom, with an "I want to become . . .", with a sense of the potentiality to become what one is not. One gropes toward this vision in the dark, with no guide, no map, and no guarantee. Here one acts as subject, author, creator.

Sometimes a process of character change may proceed with increasing momentum and finality to solid completion. The honest man becomes the complete thief; the thief becomes the completely honest man. When this occurs it is likely, not only that the old way of life has been given up, but also that a new way of life, directly opposite in implication, has been adopted. Such a change is experienced not as a deflection of course, but as an absolute turning around, a conversion, may even call for a change of name. Saul of Tarsus had such an experience on the road to Damascus and—having been the chief persecutor of Christianity—became its greatest exponent. Malcolm X had such an experience in prison with the teachings of Elijah Muhammad, and changed not simply from thief to nonthief, but from thief to social reformer; the completeness and finality with which he transcended the old identity owed as much to his having undertaken with passion and commitment to correct injustice as it did to his giving up of stealing. Had he simply "learned his lesson," decided not to steal any more, and taken a time-serving job, he may never have altogether ceased being a thief. Some of the temptation, bitterness, and envy, something of the way of thought, the attitude and outlook of a thief may have remained.

Such change as occurred in Saul or Malcolm X is rare, seems so far beyond anything we might expect to achieve by our own efforts that, when it occurs, we usually ascribe credit—to a mystic force, to a revelation, to the hand of God. Such changes as we achieve in ourselves, with or without therapy, are likely to be partial and provisional. The homosexual man gets married, has children, but never feels entirely safe with women; the frigid woman becomes capable of climax, but not easily and not always; the impotent man becomes able usually to make it, but can never be sure; the depressive character can work, may occasionally feel glad to be alive, but is not likely ever to be described as of sunny disposition; the phobic woman becomes less anxious, no longer has to decline invitations, but always has sweaty hands at cocktail parties. Such changes must be counted success; for more frequent in outcome, even with considerable effort, is no change at all. He who undertakes to transform himself, therefore, should think not of all or none, sick or well, miserable or happy, but of more or less, better or worse. He should undertake only to do what he can, to handle something better, to suffer less. The kingdom of heaven need not concern him.

When the thief takes a job and determines to go straight, when the homosexual man finds a woman and renounces sexual relations with men, he does so with a vision of what he will become. Rarely may such direct action, in the course of time and of great effort, succeed without further insight and with no change of plan. More often the course upon which one has embarked entails so much anxiety, uncertainty, confusion, that reappraisal becomes necessary. One finds that his entire self was not known, that submerged aspects of self now rise up in terror, threat, and subversion, screaming outrage, demanding revocation. One is forced to a halt, sometimes driven back. The whole issue has to be rethought. "What I'm giving up is more important than I knew." "Maybe I don't want to change." "Am I going at it the wrong way?" Newly emerging feelings and reactions must be explored in relation to other known elements and to one's now threatened intention.

Here therapy may offer insight into bewildering experience, help with the making of new connections, give comfort and encouragement, assist in the always slippery decision of whether to hang on and try harder or to look for a different way to try. That person gains most from therapy, and gains it most quickly, who has the heart and will to go it alone in the event that therapy does not help; whereas he who clings to therapy as drowning man to ship's timber is likely to burden therapy with a weight it can't support and so take himself and therapy down together.

IX

PSYCHOTHERAPY

Sometimes we suffer desperately, would do anything, try anything, but are lost, see no way. We cast about, distract ourselves, search, but find no connection between the misery we feel and the way we live. The pain comes from nowhere, gives no clue. We are bored, nothing has meaning; we become depressed. What to do? How to live? Something is wrong but we cannot imagine another way of living which would free us.

Yet there must be a way, for no sustained feeling can exist as a thing in itself, independent of what we do. If the suffering is serious and intractable it must be intimately and extensively connected, in ways we do not perceive, with the way we live. We have to look for such connections. Sometimes there is nothing to be done until they are found.

Therapy may help. One may discover, for example, a simmering hatred of one's husband or wife, not consciously felt, not expressed, but turned against one's self, experienced as depression. Such a finding may still not indicate what one should do; for that will depend on yet other feelings, connections, implications. Should one begin to express the anger? Perhaps, if the grievance is reasonable and if there is also affinity and love. Should one get a divorce? Perhaps, if there is not even that minimum affection necessary for trying to work out differences. Sometimes there is no love and good reason for hatred, and still one does not want a divorce; then one must be struck by this curious thing, that one clings to a source of frustration and torment, must ask why, and perhaps only then may begin to uncover a profound dependence which has been both well hidden by, and fully expressed in, the hostile tie. One hates the other but can't leave because one is afraid. Afraid of what? And why? What one should do may come to be known only after this dependence is examined in its relation to various other feelings and experiences. Sometimes there is no grievance and much love, and then, gradually, one may learn that he scapegoats the other and may realize that he must, therefore, be needing to feel hatred, that he is using it for ulterior purposes —perhaps to cover up feelings of inadequacy, so avoiding the awareness of what he might want to do if he weren't afraid.

Much of our suffering is just so obscure as this. Frigidity, social anxiety, isolation, boredom, disaffection with life— in all such states we may see no correlation between the inner feeling and the way we live. Yet no such feeling can be independent of behavior; and if only we find the connections we may begin to see how a change in the way we live will make for a change in what we feel.

Since freedom depends upon awareness, psychotherapy may, by extending awareness, create freedom. But not surely, and not always. When in therapy a life story is examined in such a way that what the patient knows and feels, what he remembers and can reason from, is systematically discounted, while significant causality is located only in those unconscious forces postulated by the therapist, in hidden constraints situational and libidinal which allegedly twisted him and shaped defenses, required that he react in the way he did and in no other—in all this one is rewriting the past, is taking a story which must have contained elements of freedom and responsibility and retelling it in terms only of causes lying outside awareness and hence beyond control, so teaching the patient to see himself as the passive product of inscrutable forces. Where he feels himself to be the author of action, his analysis will show him to be "acting out," that is, an object being acted upon. He may come then to regard himself as lived by unknown and unknowable forces. As consolation prize he may acquire the capacity to guess, in the current jargon, at the nature of those obscure forces which move him. But only guess, must not attempt seriously to bear witness to that which, by definition, he cannot know. He may remain then forever the dilettante, making modest conjecture at the gusts which blow him this way and that, and so become not only an object but opaque, most necessarily to himself.

A "completely analyzed" person is one who has been treated for many years by an orthodox analyst. When such a one breaks down and is hospitalized, we are surprised; if the patient is himself a psychoanalyst, we are shocked. Our reaction bespeaks the assumption that thorough analysis resolves all serious inner conflict, that thereafter —though one may expect times of sadness, uncertainty, and unrest—these will derive from reality conflicts and so will not lead to breakdown. There is little to support such a view; indeed, the most cursory glance at three generations of analysts leaves it in tatters. The surprise we feel when a "well-analyzed" person breaks down derives from our wish to view man as a machine. Very delicate and complicated, to be sure, like a fine watch, and liable therefore to subtle, tricky problems of adjustment which may require the lengthy services of an expert; but when finally we get rid of all the bugs we may expect smooth and reliable function. Such an image of man is at odds with what we know life to be. If we seriously regard our private thought and feeling, our visions at night when the wind blows, when rain falls on a deserted island, then— though fine adjustments have been made by a great watch-maker—we find so much conflict, misery, confusion, that we know we are never through and never safe. The suffering and the danger cannot be left behind. They are what we are. Psychoanalysis does not qualify anyone to live in the kingdom of heaven, only helps in the effort to change in such a way as to deal better with emerging conflicts which will never end so long as we live. Indeed, since we who undertake analysis are those who have more than average trouble with inner conflict, we may receive considerable help—quite enough to justify the undertaking

—and still end up with more misery than those who have not been analyzed.

In reconstructing a life story truth is necessary but not sufficient. Truth does not demarcate, cannot determine whether we should dwell upon cause or choice. Two histories of the same life may be radically different, yet equally true. If we have failed an examination we may say, "I would not have failed if the teacher had not asked that question on Cromwell, which, after all, had not come up in class," or "I would not have failed if I had studied harder." Both statements are addressed to the same experience, in the same effort to understand; both claim to answer the question "Why did I fail?" and both may be true. Truth does not here provide the criterion for selection; the way we understand the past is determined, rather, by the future we desire. If we want to excuse ourselves we elect the former view; if we want to avoid such failures in the future we elect the latter. (If we believe our aim to be the passing of such exams in the future, and if we nevertheless elect the former view of the present failure, then we are confused.)

Likewise in addressing ourselves to the failure of a lifetime, and asking why, we may arrive at answers significantly different but equally true. In the life most free and most aware, so much defining action still occurs without choice that it is always feasible to compose an accurate and cogent account in terms only of genes, drives, and circumstance. Conversely, in the life most crushed by outside force, there nevertheless exists the potentiality for actions other than those in fact taken. With the noose around our necks there still are options—to curse God or to pray, to weep or to slap the executioner in the face.

Of two equally true accounts of the same life the one we choose will depend upon the consequences we desire, the future we intend to create. If the life is our own or one of our patients', if it involves suffering and there is desire to change, we will elect a history written in terms of past determinism which creates present choice; for this is the view that insists upon both the understanding of how one has come to be what one is and the freedom to make one's self into something different. If the life in question is one we observe from a distance, without contact or influence, for example a life which has ended, we may elect a history written in terms only of cause. In reconstructing a life that ended at Auschwitz we usually ignore options for other courses of individual behavior, locate cause and responsibility with the Nazis; for our intent is not to appraise the extent to which one person realized existing opportunity, but to examine and condemn the social evil which encompassed and doomed him. In considering the first eighteen years of the life of Malcolm X few of us would find much point in formulating his progress from delinquency to rackets to robbery to prison in terms of choice, holding him responsible for not having transcended circumstance; most of us would find the meaning of his story to lie in the manner in which racism may be seen as the cause of his downward course.

Conflict, suffering, psychotherapy—all these lead us to look again at ourselves, to look more carefully, in greater detail, to find what we have missed, to understand a mystery; and all this extends awareness. But whether this greater awareness will increase or diminish freedom will depend upon what it is we become aware of and how we use it. If the greater awareness is of unconscious forces which are postulated as determining causes and which remain outside our experience, and if we use that understanding of the past only to prove that we "had" to become what we are, then, since this view applies equally to the present which is the unbroken extension of that determined past, therapy may become a way of establishing why we must continue to be what we have been, a way of disavowing choice with the apparent blessing of science, and the net effect will be a decrease in freedom. If, however, the determining causes of which we gain awareness lie within, or are brought within, our experience, and if we use this gain in understanding to create present options, freedom will be increased, and with it greater responsibility for what we have been, are, and will become.